PRAISE FOR *THE REGENER*

T0032184

"Carol Sanford's clear and accessible writing keeps urging us toward higher levels of organizational and self-actualization. *The Regenerative Business* blends an educator's precision guidance with a sage's wisdom and insight to deliver a roadmap for higher performance, greater impact, and long-term value creation. Her teachings bring work systems design into sharp focus, a new and essential skill set for innovative business leaders to embrace and master."

William Rosenzweig, Co-author, *The Republic of Tea: How an Idea Becomes a Business*, Oslo Business for Peace Award, UC Berkeley, Haas Business School

"The work that Carol Sanford describes in *The Regenerative Business* profoundly changed my life, and I'm confident it will change yours too. Carol's work also exponentially contributed to increasing the value of my company over the three years we worked together—that value increased by about $100 million. Carol uniquely understands how to cultivate human potential by developing more conscious, creative, innovative, and intentional human beings. You will discover purpose in your work that will drive extraordinary results. You will find that you have the ability to develop capabilities that you never dreamed of. And perhaps most important of all, you will discover that your work can be fulfilling in numerous ways that deeply feed your soul."

Jeffrey Hollender, Founder and CEO, SustainNatural. com, and Founding CEO, Seventh Generation

"*The Regenerative Business* is a passionate call to reimagine work that is rooted not only in Carol's many years as consultant to some of the most transformative companies of our time, but also in the latest research in psychology and productivity. Rather than thinking of organizations as machines and people as cogs to be manipulated, Carol advocates for a vision of firms as cradles of human development, supporting their employees through journeys of discovery that focus on the lived experience of the customer. Her work points the way to building authentically purpose-driven firms that will drive the kind of disruption that my own research suggests is likely to be catalysts in reimagining capitalism and to a way of being in the world that is simultaneously deeply pragmatic and an expression of transformative hope."

Rebecca M. Henderson, John and Natty McArthur University Professor, Harvard Business School

"Carol lays out the future of workplace design just in time for the paradigm shift we are experiencing now. She provides us with a language and methodology, tested for decades, on aligning our highest individual potential with nature's patterns to evolve our highest collective capacity. She has already influenced my own thinking and that of Kauffman leaders, and we are partnering with her for more evolution in entrepreneurship and education to great ends. It's just what the world needs to transform our fractured and fragmented workplace culture into a healthy, regenerative whole system."

Mark Beam, Maverick in Residence, Kauffman Foundation

"What I appreciated about Carol's book is that she has taken what I write about—the science of motivation in the individual and one-to-one contexts— and through her brilliant approach, shows us how to apply the science in the organization context. She demonstrates, with dozens of case stories, how to apply the concepts systemically. Why not design organizations where people thrive? Carol shows you how."

Susan Fowler, Author, *Why Motivating People Doesn't Work ... and What Does: The New Science of Leading, Energizing, and Engaging*

"Leading successful business transformation in a complex and challenging environment requires clarity, alignment, will, and a sense of purpose at all levels across the organization. The principles and ideas presented in *The Regenerative Business* deliver these effects systemically and in a way that brings deeper satisfaction and meaning to work. Carol explains her approach using real-world examples and with candor that is both clarifying and refreshing. Using her frameworks to build a developmental organization is producing significant cultural shifts that are moving our business forward. Associates are energized to grow their impact, and customers are feeling the difference."

Lara Lee, President, Orchard Supply Hardware

"Carol Sanford has deep experience helping the leadership of a diverse range of companies address pressing business challenges. Drawing on a unique embedded responsibility perspective, *The Regenerative Business* offers important new methodologies for human development and work design, aligned with strategies that ensure business and society thrive together in an increasingly complex world."

Steve Lippman, Director of Corporate Citizenship, Microsoft, Inc.

"Carol Sanford has fundamentally challenged and transformed the way we think about entrepreneurship, innovation, and developing our leaders. Since she began teaching at the school, the impact of Carol's regenerative frameworks and concepts has reached beyond the classroom. She has supported the students, faculty, and leadership to explore how the curriculum, learning community, and organization can form a seamless whole in pursuit of driving transformative change. *The Regenerative Business* is essential reading for any leader looking to design and lead a thriving twenty-first century organization."

Christer Windeløv-Lidzélius, Principal, Kaospilot, Denmark
… business and design in leadership and entrepreneurship

"Prepare to abandon all current thinking about what makes organizations great. Original, powerful, and persuasive, *The Regenerative Business* exposes the limited worldviews and minimal expectations that drive most organizations. In their place, it offers practical and insightful frameworks for creating "regenerative" processes, illustrated with successful and profitable real-world applications of these ideas. Promoting ways of seeing and being in the world that couldn't be more timely or essential, *The Regenerative Business* details frameworks that engage the whole person in the larger systems in which they operate."

Jessica Lipnack and David McConville, Co-chairs,
Board of Directors, Buckminster Fuller Institute

"Everyone is talking about the future of work. Carol Sanford offers us a clear-headed framework for how to get there, while leaving us with important questions that we need to answer for ourselves. If you're looking for a thoughtful and comprehensive guide to evolve your organization, you'll love this book."

Jonathan Raymond, Author, *Good Authority*, and CEO, Refound

"At Sustainable Brands, we are committed to being a living lab of the sustainable brand of the future. I know full well Carol is a master at applying systems thinking to smart, sustainable organizational behavior, and I can't wait to put Carol's concepts into practice at SB."

KoAnn Vikoren Skrzyniarz, Founder/CEO, Sustainable
Life Media, producers of Sustainable Brands

"Carol Sanford is one of the most interesting and unique business thinkers we know. Her approach is integral, whole, and holistic. In fact, it is the way we should run business in the twenty-first century."

Food Inspiration Magazine

"For all the talk of efficiency, modern business is grossly inefficient in developing its most valuable resource: the people who work in it. Only 13 percent of the global workforce is actively engaged by work (Gallup 2014). Carol's book offers a vision and blueprint on how to start to change that. Borrowing from deep ecology and studies of living systems, she has written a timely guide for all those (from leaders to students and everyone in between) interested in the redesign of work itself."

Manoj Fenelon, Faculty, Pratt Institute and School of Visual Arts' Design for Social Innovation Program, former Director of Innovation, Pepsico

"I have had the privilege of working with Carol Sanford over several decades, observing her wisdom and guidance catalyze businesses across the United States and Europe into profound transformations in how they worked, and the systemic value they produced. Instead of focusing on incremental improvements in existing ideas and work patterns, she moves people far upstream in their thinking to where they can rediscover their inherent, unique genius as a source of radical new creativity. In revealing the ideas and methods behind her work, *The Regenerative Business* opens a new world to business leaders who seek to make their business an agent of regeneration for their customers, employees, and communities."

Pamela Mang, Co-author of *Regenerative Development and Design: A Framework for Evolving Sustainability*, Co-founder of Regenesis Group

"Carol Sanford's new book is deep, thoughtful, and thought provoking. She challenges conventional ways of thinking about work and helps us to envision organizations in which employees are increasingly motivated, capable, and instrumental in charting the direction of the firm. Carol systematically repudiates a host of revered practices and provides an alternative structure for rethinking all aspects of how work is designed. I have known Carol for several decades and marvel at how she invites us to think much, much more systemically about how what we do at work and how we think about developing people's potential is central to making the world (and the organizations of which we are a part) better."

Pamela J. Hinds, Professor, Stanford University School of Engineering and Management Science

"Doing 'less worse' is not a goal. Imagine a healthy system and then recreate it. Carol Sanford calls us all to a higher ground and a new way of looking at organizations, and at ourselves. Technology, transparency, and data allow us to see things differently. We have learned too much about the consequences of industry to operate in the same way as before. Thanks to Carol's wise advice, we are redesigning business, using the fashion industry as our pilot, creating a respectful and regenerative ecosystem. Carol helped light the spark that ignited the Fair Fashion Center. Her spiritual consciousness and business acumen make her the ideal partner with which to reshape our thinking, our companies, and as a consequence, our world."

Cara Smyth, GCNYC Vice President and Founding
Director of the Fair Fashion Center

"If you aspire to build a developmental way of working that is able to adapt to rapidly changing market conditions and achieve disruptive, sustainable innovation, you need to read *The Regenerative Business*. Carol Sanford introduces a breakthrough methodology that will fundamentally transform your thinking and your organization. Incorporating insights from Sanford's extensive experience and a compelling writing style, this book is an indispensable resource."

Denise Lee Yohn, Author, *What Great Brands Do*

"Sanford ably weaves together a compelling book that shifts our focus from the standard technocratic, mechanistic view of the business world to a more comprehensive view that places the human being at the center. This humanistic, systems approach can truly help organizational leaders of all types drive change, while also recognizing the power of people who are the center of any organizational endeavor. In the end, *The Regenerative Business* is a critical addition to the larger body of new thinking around people-centered workplaces, change management, and disruptive innovation, pushing us to recognize Sanford's powerful point that ultimately 'the work of growing great companies turns out to be, as well, the work of growing ourselves.'"

Nathan Long, President, Saybrook University

"As the world of work becomes more global, automated, and unpredictable, Carol Sanford offers an innovative approach to innovation itself—change the way we think, invest in people, and then structure the organization to support them so the regenerative paradigm can work its magic. Grounded in theory and experience, Sanford offers compelling examples and case studies that make this a must-read for leaders everywhere."

David Livermore, PhD, author and thought leader
on global leadership and cultural intelligence

The Regenerative Business

Redesign Work, Cultivate Human Potential, and Achieve Extraordinary Outcomes

Carol Sanford

NICHOLAS BREALEY
PUBLISHING

BOSTON • LONDON

First published in 2017 by Nicholas Brealey Publishing. An Imprint of John Murray Press.

This edition published by Nicholas Brealey Publishing in 2022
An imprint of John Murray Press
A division of Hodder & Stoughton Ltd,
An Hachette UK company

1

A CIP catalogue record for this title is available from the British Library
Library of Congress Control Number: 2021949275

Trade Paperback ISBN 9781529359114
UK eBook ISBN 9781473669093
US eBook ISBN 9781473669673

Typeset in Minion Pro, Gotham Narrow & Helvetica by Jouve India.

Printed and bound in Great Britain by Clays Ltd, Elcograf S.p.A.

John Murray Press policy is to use papers that are natural, renewable and recyclable products and made from wood grown in sustainable forests. The logging and manufacturing processes are expected to conform to the environmental regulations of the country of origin.

John Murray Press   Nicholas Brealey Publishing
Carmelite House   Hachette Book Group
50 Victoria Embankment   Market Place, Center 53, State Street
London EC4Y 0DZ   Boston, MA 02109, USA

www.nbuspublishing.com

Contents

Dedication

To the brilliant leaders of regenerative business organizations with whom I have been in an astounding, reciprocal educational process for decades. Thank you all.

About the author

Photo © Kristen Imig

Carol's work is deeply rooted in the belief that people can grow and develop beyond what their leaders or anyone believes is possible: to be increasingly entrepreneurial, innovative, and responsible in their business and personal actions. For forty years, she has worked with leaders of successful companies, such as Google, DuPont, Intel, P&G, and Seventh Generation, helping them to innovate and grow their businesses by growing their people. Her work is often called ground-breaking, game changing, original, and inspiring.

Carol is currently Executive in Residence and Senior Fellow in Social Innovation at Babson College. She produces the *Business Second Opinion* podcast and the Regenerative Business Summit and Prize.

Visit her at CarolSanford.com

Foreword

Michiel Bakker, Google Food Lab

With the speed of change in the world, organizations are faced with seemingly more opportunities but also more complex interrelated challenges than ever before. How can we best ready ourselves for the world we live in today let alone tomorrow? Our success will depend on growing our individual and joint thinking capabilities and our capacity for caring. In her latest book, *The Regenerative Business: Redesign Work, Cultivate Human Potential, and Achieve Extraordinary Outcomes*, Carol Sanford builds upon her core beliefs that we all have not only the desire, but even more importantly, the opportunity to make a much bigger impact on the world and other people's lives than we even realize.

In this remarkable book, Carol writes about how to develop human talent in ways that benefit the individual, businesses, and society: an amazing win for all. She makes the case that the time has come to evolve our thinking about organizational design and structure in order to develop so much more of our human potential. What excites me so much about this book is that Carol is giving us clear guiding principles and inspiration on how to build the power, passion, and potential of people but without being prescriptive or formula driven. And that is how I come to know Carol and her books over the years. She shares fascinating and thought-provoking insights that help you further develop your own critical thinking capabilities—and, most important, your desire to act.

Carol has been and continues to be a tremendous source of inspiration for me. Through her books, many personal conversations with her over the years, and her participation in the Google Food Lab, I have become a total believer in her approach and thinking. She taught me that everything begins with you as an individual taking full responsibility for your own actions. It is about "external considering," caring for others and living things. And you must have the notion of personal agency, believing that you have a responsibility to act upon the opportunities to which you have access. If *you* don't, who will or should?

When I read Carol's first book, *The Responsible Business*, seven years ago, I was working for Starwood Hotels and Resorts. That book opened my eyes about how to engage an entire organization and all of its stakeholders in broader challenges. And to be clear, the term *organization* can be defined here in many different ways. You don't have to be a CEO to embrace and act upon the notion that in whatever you do, you have to consider the impact you make on all stakeholders of an organization. The beauty of Carol's work is that it is so relevant for everybody.

The Responsible Business became a must-read for my team members when I moved to Google in 2012 (and it still is). It is now the foundation of how we think holistically about the impact we (can) make with what we do; it is embedded in what we do. Carol's thinking was one of the sparks that enabled us to create in the fall of 2012 the Google Food Lab, a platform to engage various food system representatives in collaborative discussions about the future of food. Since joining the Google Food Lab, Carol has been contributing and sharing her insights and thinking with so many lab participants and has helped evolve both the lab's reach and impact and her own. Affecting change in food systems around the world is incredibly complex and requires the type of thinking and collaboration for which Carol so passionately advocates. I can say firsthand that one of the things that makes Carol so special is that she fully practices what she teaches.

The concepts in this newest book, *The Regenerative Business*, have already helped me evolve my thinking on people management. It has broadened my viewpoints on how to work best with people in today's environment and how you can make such a difference by designing work in ways that ignite their growth and contribution. Furthermore, Carol highlights for me the need for individuals and organizations to increase their critical thinking capabilities, a competency now more important than ever as the pace of change in the world accelerates. The book connects the dots so well between the organization, strategy execution, and culture evolution (covered in her book *The Responsible Entrepreneur*)—and now the people who are doing the work.

Unlock and maximize the potential of yourself and those you work with by enjoying this great read.

Foreword

Cheryl Kiser, Lewis Institute at Babson

It has been said many times that Carol Sanford's insights, writings, and contributions to business and society are a gift. *The Regenerative Business* is an extraordinary gift that she has given to us at a powerfully important time as we better refine and define the purpose of business. A gift for everyone who believes that the human spirit is best served when it is allowed to create and express itself authentically and in community. A gift for those who know that business needs a redesign, and a new articulation of what really drives business growth, innovation, employee engagement, and a better connection to society. And for those who know that developing and engaging the whole person on the job builds a more integrated and whole organization that is more relevant, responsible, and successful.

Thank you, Carol Sanford, on behalf of all of us in academia, business, government, and civil society who seek to influence and educate leaders of all kinds capable of creating great economic and social value simultaneously.

If only every person had exposure to your way of thinking, being, and expressing, we would universally be a *regenerative society* in which we create from a place of abundance, not scarcity. Where we awaken and more effectively tap into our desire to co-create, innovate, connect, and generate positive outcomes not just for ourselves but for others. Where the desire to contribute to something greater than ourselves unleashes our discretionary effort and spurs innovation and personal commitment to the business or organization we are part of in ways never imagined.

The Regenerative Business is an invitation to embark on a powerful journey to make much needed change. Carol is an incredible intellectual and spiritual force whose decades of business and life experiences are already altering our perspective on business and what it takes to create true value in today's marketplace.

Her stories of business transformation, positive disruptive frameworks, usage of systemic language as an activator of change, connection to things greater than oneself, intentional design for creativity as an accelerator of innovation, spirituality and connection to natural systems as vital to business, and finally stories, of creating social value without using programs like corporate social responsibility, all cause reflection on what we thought we knew about business, and why we must know how to create a regenerative business.

The Regenerative Business honors what we know to be true. *Creativity and innovation are inherent in human beings, and when they have a place to be usefully expressed, they provide the necessary energy for successful businesses and enduring societies. A regenerative business taps into this powerful source, fostering it, developing it, and harnessing it to improve life for customers and workers.*

The Regenerative Business is one of the most important books right now. The world is more unpredictable and increasingly more unknowable than ever before. We can no longer extrapolate from the experiences of the past to predict the future. Leading and managing for these uncertainties will require new mindsets, new designs, and new habits. When these uncertain conditions exist and define our new normal, the best way to navigate and create is to act, learn, and build our way forward. To activate the human urge and desire to create is the most powerful energy source we have, and Carol has brilliantly captured this essence in *The Regenerative Business*.

Gallup International has told us for years through its polls that close to 70 percent of all employees are disengaged from their work, and many of them are actively disengaged. This is a problem. A huge problem.

No matter where I go or whom I talk with in business, four persistent challenges are glaringly evident: how do we grow our business, how do we innovate, how do we engage our employees, and how do we connect to society in an authentic way to create a competitive advantage?

Carol's approach to getting there from here requires a new way of designing in order to develop people not to be great performers—although they will be—but to be exceptional co-creators who innovate, seek opportunity, and engage with society so that business becomes a far more powerful economic and social force.

The Regenerative Business not only provides a roadmap for *what we need to do* to create regenerative business, it illuminates *who we need to be* as leaders and managers to make it happen.

Again, huge gratitude to Carol Sanford for helping Babson open the aperture on its view of what business can and should be. As its founder, Roger Babson, once said and as Carol calls forth in all of us today, "[We] inspire in students the will to make business an agent for the advancement of the good of the state . . . Men who combined business acumen with this higher purpose can serve their day and generation as vitally and nobly as the greatest statesmen, educators, preachers, and poets."

Acknowledgements

I LOVE CREATING BOOKS to tell the stories of great businesses. I love ideas that matter and can change the course of history. I have been blessed to advance a powerful theoretical basis for such change, and I have collaborated in the creation of many new startups and the redesign of Fortune 500 businesses, from initial strategizing to operational work design.

My books are great because courageous business leaders trusted and valued me as a full creative partner in processes of whole systems change. I tell real-life change stories from firsthand experience. My role has always been that of consultative educator and co-creative designer of strategic thinking, leadership and culture change, and organizational work design with people throughout all of each business.

Each of the leaders I worked with believed in the potential of every person in their business to grow beyond anything they ever thought possible. Each business moved from *buying* to *building* talent. Without exception, they learned from experience that every human being, not just a special few, is capable of creativity and innovation—of becoming a full player in the radical transformation of business outcomes.

I thank the almost one hundred leaders I have worked with in the past four decades, creating change, cultivating human potential, and achieving extraordinary results. I especially honor a few that I have stayed close to over the years, continuing to learn from and support one another: Will Lynn at Kingsford Charcoal, Britta, Deer Park, Hidden Valley Ranch, KC Masterpiece, and Hunt Wesson businesses, among others; Stelios Tsezos at Colgate Europe and Africa; Jeffrey Hollender of Seventh Generation and Sustain Natural; and Michiel Bakker of Google Food Lab.

The co-creative partners who go with me from first idea to manuscript are my longtime team: Ben Haggard, Kit Brewer, Shannon Murphy, and Tamara Packer. Many thanks to you all. I'll see you again soon for book four.

I have a newfound book creation and strategy team lead by Alicia Simmons, and I always count on Barbara Cave Henricks of Cave Henricks Communications, a media relations and book publicity expert, and my friend. I love my new editor, Alison Hankey, whose professionalism makes all of our work together fun, and my new publisher, Nicholas Brealey Publishing.

Also by Carol Sanford

The Responsible Business: Reimagining Sustainability and Success (Jossey-Bass, 2011)

The Responsible Entrepreneur: Four Game-Changing Archetypes for Founders, Leaders, and Impact Investors (Jossey-Bass, 2014)

Introduction: Pursue Disruptive Innovation

When you change the way you look at things, the things you look at change.

Max Planck, Quantum Theorist and Nobel Laureate

THESE DAYS, the idea of disruptive innovation is a hot topic among business leaders of every stripe. Many are coming to believe that disruption is core to their longevity and market position in a fast-changing world. Customers expect the companies they buy from to be on top of what's evolving in their environments and to help them address the emerging challenges and aspirations that they are discovering. Many companies complain that customers are fickle, but actually they are engaged in a process of ongoing change, just like the world around them. A well-developed capacity for innovation is the way that modern companies get out ahead of continual change.

When it's done well, disruptive innovation has the power to regenerate whole industries and markets. Beyond this, it also has the potential to regenerate the social and ecological systems within which an industry operates. This kind of innovation requires what I call *enlightened disruption*—and it takes courage. It calls for leadership that lives on the edge and is willing to introduce changes that reinvent the game for all of the businesses within an industry.

Unfortunately, most businesses work on innovation in entirely wrongheaded ways. In general, they focus exclusively on innovating their product offerings. Instead of designing new ways to work that lead naturally to great products, they seek out how-to templates offered by so-called experts. This severely limits the scope and significance of potential innovation, and it leaves companies dependent on outside expertise as the templates they adopt become outdated.

From my perspective, the potential for disruptive innovation exists in every aspect of a business, not just in its offerings. It is possible and important to innovate with regard to management, production, distribution, customer relations, marketing, supply system, investment, and at least a hundred other arenas. Foundational to all of these is innovation with regard to how organizations develop their people.

Human development builds a company's capacity to generate the thinking that will evolve its operations, industry, society, and world. Designing work systems to grow this capability in every member of the organization is essential. This, I believe, is the only way to create a business that consistently produces enlightened, disruptive innovation in a fast-changing world.

Regeneration is a process by which people, institutions, and materials evolve the capacity to fulfill their inherent potential in a world that is constantly changing around them. This can only be accomplished by going back to their roots, their origins, or their foundings to discover what is truly singular or essential about them. Bringing this essential core forward in order to express it as new capacity and relevance is another way to describe the activity of regeneration. In other words, regeneration is the means by which enlightened, disruptive innovation happens.

Disruption takes know-how, which has to be grown into an organization. That is why this book focuses on work design. More specifically, it focuses on work design that intentionally develops people's capacities and capabilities. A regenerative business grows its members, every single one of them, into innovators with a shared commitment to bring forward radically disruptive ideas. It also grows the capability of its members to *think like CEOs*, with clear enough understanding of markets and strategy to ensure that every new idea is not only compelling in its own right but also has the power to advance the company as a whole. When these complementary conditions are present, a business becomes a pipeline for innovation. This is the way to create a powerhouse, an organization that is fast, flexible, resilient, and unique enough to keep pace with the twenty-first century.

The Regenerative Mindset

At this point, you may be wondering, "Well, it sounds good, but why isn't everybody already doing it?" In practice, there are some real and not-so-obvious challenges built into creating regenerative organizations. The single greatest barrier to innovation is our unconscious attachment to comfortable and habitual patterns of thought—that is, to our mindsets. These mechanical habits are precisely why we find ourselves stuck with borrowed ideas, unable to generate anything profoundly creative and new.

How then do we learn to cultivate the unique qualities of thinking that are required for a regenerative innovation process? How do we become masters of innovative thinking, so that we are able to innovate the process itself? In my experience, we must each start by becoming aware of our mindsets and the effects they have on how we think and what we think about. By working to make ourselves conscious of these effects, we can develop the ability to choose and evolve our mindsets, which will enable us to proactively create the thinking that we will need for regenerative business practice.

A mindset is a lens through which we view and make sense of the world. It determines what we can see, how we make sense of what we see, and how we act. For example, if we envision the world as a machine, then it becomes very easy to see humans and other living systems as interchangeable cogs. In fact, this particular mindset has shaped many of the ways businesses, sciences, and governments have been organized for at least two centuries.

One of the subtle hazards associated with mindsets is that they can be the source of a host of problems. For example, one of the reasons people hang onto the machine mindset is that it has enabled us to build efficient systems for the creation and distribution of products. However, it has also generated dehumanized workplaces, damaged ecosystems, and loss of local cultures around the world. To paraphrase Albert Einstein, these problems cannot be solved with the same mechanical mindset that created them.

In business, the regenerative mindset is actually quite rare. Yet the capacity for disruptive innovation depends on the ability to see the world through precisely this lens. To create and continue to evolve a world-changing business, the regenerative mindset must be intentionally built in, not unconsciously designed out.

Consolidated Diesel

Again, it's essential to note that there is more to the idea of enlightened disruption than just bringing breakthrough products to market. A regenerative organization also shakes up the status quo in ways that make it possible to build new social systems, new capabilities for critical thinking and engagement, and new energy for democratic institutions.

I know from experience that all of this can be accomplished through the skillful practice of work design. Let me describe for you a startup that I worked on in the early 1980s, where I learned firsthand the power of regenerative business.

Consolidated Diesel Company, a joint venture between Cummins Engine and J.I. Case, was formed to build small engines for an array of consumer and industrial applications. When the startup team received the charter to create a new, state-of-the art manufacturing business, they quickly realized that it would also need to be a state-of-the-art operation with regard to how it worked with people. I was part of the team of consultants that helped them determine how to step up to these challenges.

We began by developing an inspiring direction: to usher in a new era of engines that were of such high quality that the most demanding customers in the world (at that time, Japanese manufacturers) would insist on using them in their own products. To achieve this, we committed to connecting every employee as directly as possible to the customers. "The customer's dream guides every decision we make!" became our motto.

Within a year and a half of its launch, Consolidated Diesel had distinguished itself as the world's leading manufacturer of small engines. Japanese manufacturers quickly recognized and took advantage of the superiority of its products, and they were followed soon after by manufacturers in the West. In particular, companies in the United States were drawn by the fact that Japanese imports were entering the country with American engines in them. Beginning with motorcycle engines, Consolidated Diesel quickly branched out to make products for almost any function that required a small engine: everything from lawn mowers to farm equipment.

The company's workers were completely self-managing; we never could come up with a good reason to have supervisors. Instead, on-site experts with deep experience in manufacturing provided the operator teams with the information and education they needed to act in ways that would evolve the capacity of their customers. Every member of the organization became an active cocreator of every aspect of management, from strategy to hiring to pay system to customer service.

This nonhierarchical structure was backed up with a strong culture. Every employee was expected to develop a profound understanding of what would strategically increase customers' successes. Based on this, they were encouraged to take on critical responsibilities and challenges beyond their own current capability and then grow into them. This created a cohesive spirit, as everyone pulled together to achieve something that would truly benefit the users of their products.

What made this success even more extraordinary was that the business was located in rural North Carolina, a society deeply divided by racism. One of the startup design team's explicit objectives was to adopt new business practices that would dismantle racism within Consolidated Diesel, its parent companies, and its suppliers. The team identified five key areas—including hiring and promotion—where discrimination usually occurred, and then they established principles and practices that would disrupt the subjective, often unconscious biases that went into decision making. They also placed strong emphasis on transparency, so that it was possible to challenge any decision that might be interpreted as discriminatory. This emphasis on transparency was carried into the design of the facility, which used glass walls to define private work or meeting areas. The results were immediate and profound, and they soon spread beyond the company. Employees developed a training program for Consolidated Diesel's suppliers that was based on their own growing expertise; it successfully broke down deeply engrained patterns of discrimination.

Consolidated Diesel's accomplishments turned out to be enduring. Twenty years after the start-up, I read a cover article in *Fast Company* magazine that touted the revolutionary nature of the company's work design.[1] I still see the work we did together cited from time to time in books and magazines. As my first massive work-design effort, Consolidated Diesel represented a steep learning curve for me. Now, more than three decades and one hundred organizational designs later, I've been able to deepen and significantly evolve my understanding of what it takes to create regenerative businesses.

Throughout this book, I will share my discoveries about the business practices that are fundamental to becoming regenerative in how we work. They represent my best effort to understand what makes people whole, creative, and capable of making valuable contributions to successful businesses. Insofar as these discoveries are universal, they are also true about me and about you, the reader. Consequently, the work of growing great companies turns out to be, as well, the work of growing ourselves. I invite you to join me in this process of discovery.

Who Is This Book For?

Most people spend 60 percent of their waking lives at work, which is the cornerstone of our society and our economy. Consequently, we ought to have work that works well. This book is written for people who want to design new and better ways of working: ways that address the preponderance of dissatisfaction that most people experience with their work.

When I use the term *design*, I refer to the act of intentionally generating something new, something that responds creatively to the specific needs and opportunities of a business, its customers, and its employees.

I do not mean implementing yet another off-the-shelf, currently popular program of the week. For this reason, I focus on the overarching principles and criteria that designers need to hold consciously in mind, whether they are setting up brand new companies or redesigning venerable institutions with many generations of success under their belts.

My emphasis on principles and criteria, rather than prescriptive recipes, is deliberate. My aim is to grow a higher level of discernment and creative thinking into the practice of work design, and offering another book that simply tells people what to do would undermine this intention. My hope is that readers will find this book stimulating and challenging, a pointer to the path we need to take if we are to harmonize the needs of businesses with those of their markets and of society as a whole.

This is a book for people who love the ability of businesses to foster innovation and creativity by unleashing the inherent intelligence of everyone involved. Unfortunately, business education and corporate cultures continually reinforce the idea that supporting the people in an organization comes at the expense of profitability. But with a number of pioneering business leaders, I've been able to demonstrate again and again that the opposite is true. Not only can leaders tap into the intelligence of their people as a way to grow powerfully profitable businesses, but also they can grow this intelligence to make their businesses disruptive and therefore non-displaceable and future-proof in their chosen markets.

Are you a pioneering business leader, a decision maker who is responsible for setting direction in your organization or for designing and implementing the way people work? Then I want this book to help you build financial success while blowing the roof off the creative potential of your team.

Overview

This book is divided into three sections. Part 1 provides an orientation to regenerative work design—what it is, why it matters, and how it addresses the business challenges of the twenty-first century. It describes the core characteristics of a regenerative approach and the paradigm shift this approach represents with regard to human development and disruptive innovation.

Part 2 provides the basis for assessing your business and its work design. What are its practices, where did they come from, and what are the hidden consequences of using them? For anyone who wants to create a regenerative business organization, this assessment is critical. A regenerative approach is not something that you just add on to everything you're already doing. It requires a radical re-envisioning of what business is and how it works. Thus, the first step to evolving your business is to create a plan for cleaning house, eliminating and replacing old practices that no longer serve you. (An obvious example might be replacing performance reviews and incentive programs, which are increasingly recognized as toxic practices, without bringing in something equally destructive.)

Part 3 lays out five necessary phases that your business will move through as it grows into a regenerative organization. It provides tested concepts and guidance for creating a work design that enables you to attract and keep great people, generate extraordinary financial returns, and contribute to a better society. Rather than promoting a one-size-fits-all approach, it offers a framework for stimulating your own creativity with regard to the unique conditions of your business, so that the work design you generate will be yours and yours alone.

Free download: Supplemental materials to help start your business's regenerative work design are available at *www.CarolSanford.com/ bookdownloads.*

CHAPTER ONE

Go Beyond Training and Develop Your People

Between stimulus and response there is a space. In that space is our power to choose our response. In our response lies our growth and our freedom.

Victor Frankl, *Man's Search for Meaning*

CREATIVITY AND INNOVATION are inherent in human beings. When people have a place to express these qualities in useful ways, they provide the necessary energy for successful businesses and enduring societies. Regenerative businesses tap into creativity and innovation—fostering them, developing them, and harnessing them to improve life for customers and workers. These businesses inspire employees to use their initiative to create systemic effects that ripple out and improve communities, landscapes, and nations. This becomes possible when businesses change their frames of reference, refocusing their people on understanding the customer's world so that they can discover unique ways to transform it. It is this focus on transformative effects for customers that enables regenerative businesses to disrupt their industries and markets.

At the same time, businesses that foster initiative and self-management change forever the way employees look at the world and their role within it. When people spend their lives in hierarchical systems, with supervisors making decisions for them, their decision-making capacity and their confidence in their own judgment weaken. They become habituated to ceding control and responsibility to authority figures. In the long run, this undermines not only our businesses, but our democracy and the citizenry needed to make it work. By evolving the natural sources of human creativity and responsibility, a regenerative business builds more than itself. It grows better citizens and, as a result, it builds a better nation and a better world.

The process of developing people must be built into the design of a business and how it works. It is not something that gets bolted on, along with other management practices that have accumulated over the years. Rather, it is fundamental—a necessary part of what it takes to grow a successful, holistic, highly intelligent organization.

Developing People in a Changing World

The way most companies manage their workforces is bad for business. Not coincidentally, it's also bad for people and for democracy, reinforcing inequity and alienation from social and democratic processes. This is because it draws on outmoded and inaccurate beliefs about human nature and what it takes to create healthy patterns of social engagement. For example, most managers believe that humans need to be stimulated with incentives, rewards, and recognition if they are to become motivated. Such beliefs contradict a growing body of scientific research that points to the direct connection between human agency and personal and collective motivation.[1,2] In other words, most businesses are designed to severely limit people's ability to stay motivated. Clearly, there is plenty of room for innovation.

A host of new discoveries in the fields of neuroscience and psychology have overturned long-held assumptions about human motivation and development, suggesting that we have far more capacity for free will and autonomy than has been generally assumed.[3,4] Multiple studies demonstrate that we have a stronger tendency to feel rewarded by altruism than by selfishness. We have the ability to work independently, outside the influence of our peers, if we have the opportunity to develop this capacity. With adequate support, we can learn to manage increasingly difficult and complex situations over our entire lifetime.[5] These insights directly contradict many of the core beliefs that have shaped the design and management of businesses for more than a hundred years.

The need to rethink these outmoded beliefs and replace the toxic management practices and work systems that have developed from them is becoming urgent. Automation and artificial intelligence are expected to displace 50 percent of what's left of blue-collar jobs in the U.S. by the end of this decade, part of a global phenomenon that is rapidly replacing industrial labor with machines.[6] At the same time, there is a global shortage of workers with the critical-thinking skills, technical agility, motivation, and independence needed by the emerging economy. Elon Musk, in a joint presentation with Bill Gates at the 2017 Davos World Economic Forum, pointed out that these qualities can and should be developed rapidly within the workplace and that it is in each business's interest to do so.[7] What is urgently needed now is an approach to work design that educates workers to be successful in the twenty-first century.

Not surprisingly, many members of the millennial generation are directly challenging traditional modes of doing business, which increasingly strike them as innately wrongheaded. Because of the open and transparent nature of the Internet, they have grown up with a voice and the ability to question almost anything. They don't assume that their elders know more than they do, and this is creating tensions and chaos within old-style hierarchical organizations.[8]

Also, the U.S. is experiencing a profound demographic shift as it moves from several hundred years of white majority to a pluralistic society in which people of color make up the majority. This means that a large percentage of the workforce is growing up in cultural milieus that differ from what has been the white mainstream. As communities of color become more central to the future of businesses, they expect their values to be reflected in the workplace.[9]

These phenomena are part of a larger social shift toward increasing dissatisfaction with top-down decision making. Across the political spectrum, people are insisting on their own autonomy and resisting the imposition of governmental or corporate institutions. The Tea Party, Occupy Wall Street, Black Lives Matter, and the homeschooling movements are all manifestations of a revolutionary impulse that harkens back to the founding of the U.S., when the colonies shook off the dominance of a British ruling class.

This impulse is creating enormous stresses in both government and business, and organizations of all sorts are scrambling to respond. However, most of the currently available solutions that are focused on creating greater autonomy and less bureaucracy fail to address one essential, underlying problem: our social institutions have fostered an impulse toward greater freedom but have failed to equip citizens with the corresponding critical-thinking capabilities to use that freedom effectively. The good news here is that this failure represents an unprecedented opportunity for businesses. If they can develop these capabilities in their workforces, they will strengthen not only themselves but also democracy as a whole.

Traditional ways of running a business and managing its people act against the development, full expression, and contribution of human beings. As a rule, they are grounded in a belief that human potential is fixed at birth, an accident of genetic or socioeconomic background. People must therefore be slotted into appropriate positions within hierarchical systems, and those who are smarter must naturally make decisions for everyone else.

Recognizing that there is room for innovation, a number of businesses and the consultants who serve them have worked hard to create flat organizations with self-directed employees. But unfortunately, many of these alternative structures are still based on the old belief about motivation— namely, that it is fostered through a system of rewards and punishments. Also, many of them focus on the development of technical skills, rather than on the deep work of growing critical thinking, personal mastery, and business acumen.

In fact, everyone has an inherent capacity not only to develop new skills, but also to become smarter and more capable of taking on larger and larger challenges. Businesses are in an exceptionally leveraged position to develop this capacity because it is in their best interest to do so. Specifically, businesses should strive to provide people with increasingly significant challenges that they can use to grow themselves, along with an unswerving commitment to help them develop the requisite critical-thinking skills and ability to manage themselves.

The technology for developing people in this way has been around for more than fifty years, the result of a lifelong collaboration between my mentors James V. Clark and Charles G. Krone. Krone was a philosopher with a degree in chemical engineering, while Clark was a Harvard-trained specialist in educational psychology. Their pioneering work at Proctor and Gamble in the 1960s helped introduce the world to the practice of regenerative business design.[10] Their work, and the work of their students and colleagues, has demonstrated time and again that the development of people is a powerfully effective way to build successful businesses and healthy communities.

Yet although regenerative business design is powerful and proven, it has not been widely understood or adopted. This is because it requires the deep examination of a business's starting premises and what it is willing to undertake. It also requires embracing the internal destabilization and discomfort that come with responding creatively to the unknown. The payoff is a motivated and innovative workforce that is prepared to take a company to the top of its industry.

By tapping into the inherent, self-organizing, creative energies of your workforce, you will improve margins, cash flow, and earnings. As an added bonus, you will contribute to making better lives for the people your business affects and more enduring democratic institutions for society as a whole.

Building the Capacity for Disruptive Thinking

Disruption, in the context of business, refers to the introduction of a new product or way of working that has the effect of overturning existing patterns within an industry. Disruptive innovations arise when a company looks beyond what currently exists to what *wants* to exist. Such a company learns to see what others can't see—the emergent patterns and tendencies of an evolving world.

Disruption bypasses existing dysfunctional patterns in a system, patterns that produce more negative side effects than they do benefits. It sets out to create an alternative prototype that is consistent with the system's deeper intentions or aspirations. Elon Musk describes intentional disruption as "going back to first principles."[11]

Going back to first principles allows people to make a new start. Perhaps the simplest way to describe a regenerative process is to say that it breaks a familiar pattern by going back to the original source in order to start down a different path. From this new path, people are able to make connections that they haven't made before because they're seeing the world in a new way. By disrupting the old view and its attendant certainties, by questioning everything, they can take an imaginative leap into what doesn't exist yet but will come to be when they find a way to provide the necessary conditions.

In order to create disrupting innovations, we have to break our habits of mind—how we make sense of life. To innovate in human work requires us to reframe the way we work, conceive of life, and interpret human nature.

A Parable about Growing People Regeneratively

The powerful impact of disruption and regeneration is evident even in everyday life, depending on the mindset we bring to observation. An example is an intervention I was invited to make in the lives of a young mother and her daughter, which had the effect of regenerating their relationship.

Some years ago I was teaching a course to young parents in my community who were struggling with basic child-rearing skills. A friend had pointed out that the work I was doing with businesses also applied in the arena of parenting and asked if I would be willing to share my approach as a community service. I thought this was an intriguing idea, so I gave it a try. It turned out that educating parents was identical to educating business executives.

One of my students, a woman named Nancy, had come to me for assistance with her twelve-year-old daughter, Jane. She was worried because Jane was beginning to misbehave in ways that reminded Nancy of her own troubled childhood. I asked her to tell me about the problems she was encountering and what she was doing to address them. She reported that Jane talked back, refused to do what she was asked, and was impolite in social settings.

From my perspective these sounded like fairly normal adolescent behaviors, so I pressed Nancy for more details. She admitted that there were other worrisome signs: Jane was cutting herself and manifesting early symptoms of eating disorders. Nancy was afraid for her daughter. She believed that these were indications that her child was headed down a bad path and needed immediate correction. She critiqued Jane and instituted punishments: "You won't be able to go out with your friends if you don't complete your homework." She caught herself yelling and struggled to tone down her reactions. In other words, she saw her daughter's behavior as a problem and she was in full problem-solving mode.

I wanted to shift her perspective away from being a problem parent with a problem child, so I asked her if there were things she had discovered that were working. She reported that when she could find activities to share with her daughter, the relationship improved. Jane liked mysteries, so Nancy brought her novels from the library and they read and talked about them together. They liked baking and enjoyed inventing new cookie recipes. These shared activities built Jane's confidence and engaged her in a positive relationship with her mother.

My question moved Nancy to think about what's involved in good parenting, releasing her from the trap of endless problem solving. From this perspective, she could see that she was attempting to model an ideal mother-daughter relationship and that Jane was responding positively.

From this juncture, I was able to introduce a line of questioning that evoked potential for both mother and daughter. I began with the question, "When does Jane get really excited and fully engaged in what she's doing?" This was an easy question for Nancy to answer.

"When she gets to be theatrical. She writes little plays and puts them on with her friends. She stages them and invites people to come see them. It's as though she's working through the big questions in her life through theater." The effect of this shift to Jane's deepest interest was immediate. Nancy brightened. I asked her to reflect on what had just happened.

"I went from pulling thorny weeds to nurturing a precious seed."

"How would you describe that seed?" I asked.

"Well, it's the seed of a storyteller!"

"Any particular kind of story?"

"Yes, she writes stories about her own life. I can see her understanding of life unfolding as she works on them. It even has that effect on her friends."

"So we now know something about Jane's authentic self. What brings her alive is the ability to tell growth-inducing stories, stories that reveal the struggles we encounter as we seek to create our own lives."

Nancy paused before she replied, a little dumbfounded. "How could I have been missing this for so long? It's so obvious."

I pressed her gently, "Well, then, what would Jane say she needs to express herself authentically? What aspiration is she holding?"

"She would say that she wants to be a better writer. She's very self-critical, and it makes it hard for her to keep moving because she judges herself as she's trying to write."

"In what way could you be a resource to her around this?"

"I could help her find a writing coach. There are great people in our area. I just need to find one who's willing to work with a twelve-year-old."

"So it's possible to work on what's good and ideal, but it needs to start from what Jane is pursuing and not from what we as parents, or as a culture at large, think she should be pursuing."

Nancy nodded her head.

"We can still work on problem solving, but now we can look at the process from Jane's perspective. What problems would she identify that prevent her from attaining her vision? These may be different than the ones you believe she should work on."

Nancy thought about this. "Well, I can see that what I was describing as Jane being socially inappropriate really comes from her inability to sit still and focus. But that's also her main challenge when it comes to writing. And she would immediately agree with that."

"So let's reflect on our conversation. What's the difference between how you were working on being a mother to Jane and what you're seeing now?"

"I need to remember what brings her alive. Because when I don't, my actions put me in conflict with her. They don't start from what's important to her."

Out of this conversation, Nancy was able to see ways to join with her daughter in support of a deep and ongoing process of self-development. She took Jane to buy stage makeup and found her a small movie camera to record her productions. Her view of what it means to be a good parent underwent a profound transformation. Instead of trying to fix what was broken and provide a good role model, Nancy saw that her daughter was a unique person on a unique path and that she could support her in what she was striving to become.

About ten years later, I attended a children's theater production in which the daughter of a friend was performing. The children had written and produced their own short plays about life lessons they had encountered. Something struck me as familiar about this, and I checked my program for the name of the project director. Sure enough, it was Jane, who was now a young adult.

General Themes from This Parable

Nancy and Jane's story illustrates seven important qualities of regenerative processes:

- Wholeness
- Potential
- Reciprocity
- Authenticity
- Nestedness

- Nodal intervention
- Development of capability

Here is how they showed up in Nancy's unfolding realization.

Wholeness

Nancy had fallen into the habit of labeling her daughter as a rebellious adolescent rather than seeing her as Jane. This caused her to narrow in on Jane's behavior, which was making it difficult to relate to the *whole* of Jane's being. My intervention gently reminded her of this and shifted her to a new perspective from which she was able to find ways to move the relationship forward.

Every human is a *whole* being, but we have a strong tendency to see people only in terms of those characteristics or traits that are immediately apparent to us. This person is nice, that person is old, another is high functioning, and yet another is mentally ill. But each of these descriptors is partial; none speaks to the whole person.

Potential

A critical and often overlooked aspect of any living thing's wholeness is its *potential*. At one level, Nancy's observations about her daughter's behavior were accurate. They were, after all, coming out of her direct day-to-day experience. But they were also colored by fear and her own personal history. By reconnecting to Jane's potential, Nancy was able to look beyond the apparent problems and focus on working together creatively. As a mother, this kind of knowing was as available to Nancy as the evidence of her senses. But it was not something that she had been taught to look for.

Reciprocity

Through the process described in this story, Nancy was able to enter into a much more *reciprocal* relationship with her daughter, thereby helping Jane build the capacity to be in a reciprocal relationship with her world. Rather than trying to bend Jane to her will, extracting compliance from her through punishments or rewards, Nancy was able to define a larger domain, playwriting, which would require effort from each of them. The improvements in Jane's ability to manage herself were byproducts of her motivation to master a creative endeavor that she was passionate about.

Authenticity

Recognizing Jane's *authentic self* gave Nancy the insight she needed to reverse the mutually degenerative spiral they had been locked into together. Through it Nancy was able to see Jane whole and filled with potential. She was able to discover a path by which Jane could develop herself, organized around enabling her to make the distinctive contribution she was called to.

Nestedness

Nancy might not have been persuaded that this approach would be powerfully successful if it were not for the fact that she could see that it was *nested* organically in Jane's social world. Jane was not the only troubled adolescent in her circle. She was skilled at giving voice to her struggles and was able to engage her peers in ways that enabled them to participate in working out their own conflicts. As an adult, she continued to place this ability in service to her community in order to help the next generation of young people.

Nodal Intervention

When Nancy realized that she needed to help Jane learn how to write, she discovered the appropriate *nodal intervention* that would unleash her daughter's potential. Jane was a natural storyteller, but she didn't have the discipline or the training to create the structure that would enable her to powerfully communicate her feelings and ideas to others. By addressing this critical restraint, Nancy intuited that Jane could tap into the energy that would fuel her ability to grow and mature as a person and an artist.

Development of Capability

Until this moment, Jane had struggled to manage her own emotions, turning them in rather extreme ways against herself, her mother, and the people she encountered. By offering her a structured opportunity to build her skills as a writer, Nancy was creating the context within which Jane could *develop her own capability* for self-management and critical thinking.

This was the crucial lesson for Nancy. As Jane increasingly organized her life and activities around the work she was passionate about, she began to grow and thrive. Nancy could clearly see the development in her daughter, development that was driven by Jane's own nature and energy. Prior to this, Nancy had tried in haphazard ways to shift Jane's behaviors by manipulating or containing her. Now Nancy was working intentionally to provide Jane with everything she needed to pursue her own potential.

I encountered Nancy and Jane at a moment of crisis in their relationship, a crisis that was resolved in a particularly beneficial way. However, it is important to recognize that what came out of this intervention was not a one-time course correction. Rather, it laid a groundwork that enabled both mother and daughter to revisit and deepen their understanding of these themes through time. Authenticity, potential, and inner development are qualities that require ongoing engagement through the course of a lifetime. This is how people regenerate themselves and—in the process—bring new meaning and possibility into their lives and the world.

CHAPTER TWO

The Evolution of Work Design

Regeneration goes beyond resilience or sustainability.[1]
Whatever is resilient, restored, robust, or sustainable resists
or recovers from shocks and stays the same. Shocks make a
regenerative business better. It rebounds by building the capac-
ity to do and be more than it was before.

Carol Sanford, inspired by Nassim Nicholas Taleb, Author

BUSINESSES AROUND THE WORLD have entered a rich and turbulent era of experimentation. For a host of reasons, old models of command and control have been challenged and partially dismantled, but they have yet to be replaced by fully coherent, functional alternatives. A regenerative approach offers a way forward, providing a comprehensive view of what businesses can become when they return to fundamental principles in order to start down new paths.

Work design is the key to developing people who have the ability to create a regenerative business. It is the way an organization creates the necessary conditions for its people to accomplish a collective purpose, and in particular it is a business's functional foundation, the means by which it organizes itself to get work done. Unless people think about how to work together, it's difficult for them to coordinate activities, and it's almost impossible for them to evolve the ability to perform sophisticated actions requiring the integration of multiple skills and disciplines. Work design addresses everything from decision-making processes to reporting relationships to pay and promotion to how people get hired and managed. When practiced at the highest levels of skill and imagination, it becomes an art of evoking motivation.

There are many additional reasons why a business engages in work design. For example, if customers expect consistency and reliability, then a business needs to know how it's going to deliver those results. The larger and more diversified a business becomes and the more people who become involved, the greater the need for some way of coordinating diverse efforts. If a business wants to differentiate itself and not do the same things in the same way that everyone else is doing them, it needs to give conscious attention to how it's working and what it's working on. And finally, if a business wants to be a great place to work and make a meaningful contribution to society and the world, then it must explore ways of working that are capable of producing these outcomes.

Unfortunately, the majority of work design is generic, haphazard, and cobbled together out of a hodgepodge of best practices. When this is the case, a business undermines its own success, sacrificing the larger social contributions that are the hallmark of greatness. Even worse, bad work design relegates human beings to activities that are repetitive, uncreative, unrewarding, and spirit killing.

The alternative is to design businesses from a unified and systemic philosophy of human development. The regenerative approach to work design begins from the recognition that human beings share certain fundamental characteristics:

- They have an innate desire to grow and improve.
- They are social and benefit from opportunities to engage with and learn from one another.
- They derive a sense of meaning and purpose from contributing to something larger than themselves.

A regenerative business elicits and strengthens all three of these characteristics in its employees and builds them into the core of its operations.

Coherence by Design

Research on work design and management practice draws from disciplines as diverse as psychology, engineering, and education. In recent years, there has been a proliferation of cross-disciplinary investigation into motivation, worker health, change theory, innovation, human development, and productivity. This has yielded abundant data, but this data tends to be fragmented and thus applied in piecemeal ways.

What's missing is a way to bring these diverse streams of thought and research together in a systemic relationship. Without this, organizations tend to cherry-pick small, apparently manageable pieces that appear to fill some perceived gap and attempt to force these pieces into their existing cultures and operations. As a friend of mine used to say, they "beat them to fit and paint them to match." Needless to say, this approach rarely works, either because it overlooks one or more critical dimensions or because it introduces foreign practices that are incompatible with the organization's culture. A new idea becomes just another program of the month: try it, watch it fail, spit it out.

A regenerative approach to work design is powerful precisely because it provides a coherent worldview and a framework for integrating all dimensions of human and business development. By adopting a systems regeneration mindset, this approach offers a highly sophisticated way to tie questions of motivation and self-management to the contributions a business makes to its stakeholders. A regenerative work design is never off the shelf. It is grown from fundamental principles by the people in an organization in a way that is consistent with their own unique nature and purpose.

Three Approaches to Work Design

Ideas about work design have evolved over many decades, reflecting growing understanding of the natural world and of human dynamics. And as they have evolved, so has the focus of the work designer. Initially, work design focused on *performance improvement*, or how well a business and all of its people were performing with regard to serving its customers. It has since become apparent that when performance is the primary concern, the scope of design tends to be narrow, limited mostly to efficient functioning.

The beginning of the second half of the twentieth century saw the emergence of a new focus on *human growth*. This grew out of the human potential movement, cognitive psychology, and breakthroughs in neuroscience. These streams of thought greatly enriched the growing understanding of how to provide meaningful work to an empowered workforce. The scope of work design expanded to include the facilitation of people's ability to work together as part of creative, self-directing teams.

In parallel with the development of an approach that focused on human growth, a third stream of thinking explored the implications of theories of complex living systems for work design. This approach made *systems regeneration* its primary concern and considerably broadened the focus of work design to include the improvement of all of the multiple, overlapping socioecological systems that a business is part of. This provided the basis for building regenerative businesses.

Each of these approaches—representing three historical eras in the evolution of work design—can be found in the business world today (although systems regeneration is by far the least common). They can also be described through a simple diagram, which shows them nested one inside the other.

Three Approaches to Work Design

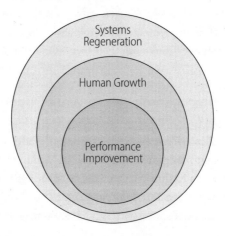

This depicts a progression in which each approach incorporates the outcomes and concerns of its predecessor, while taking into account a larger scope of variables and possibilities.

Work Design for Performance Improvement

Early in my career, I worked with Gary Gift, a business unit leader at a Fortune 500 technology company. He asked a question that startled and amused me—although every manager I've worked with since has asked the same question: "What do I do about people who just don't want to change? They know what they're good at and that's what they do. They're not interested in going beyond what their job description calls for."

"That's interesting," I responded. "Can you tell me who they are?"

"Well, there are a lot of people like that."

"Okay, but be specific. Make a list of everyone you're absolutely sure won't change."

That was harder than he expected, but eventually he was able to do it.

"Now put this list in an envelope and seal it," I said, "and we'll open it in six months."

After six months of our work together, he opened his envelope. As I had quietly suspected, many of the people he had assumed would be most resistant were now leading profound change efforts within his organization. Some of them reported that they had been waiting for years for the opportunity to take on something that would actually be meaningful.

In that moment, Gift could see that his mindset, including his preconceived notions about how people react to change, had not only limited his own perception, rendering it inaccurate, but also created an environment that locked his people into patterns that served neither them nor the company.

Gift's organization had developed a culture that was primarily focused on performance improvement. As part of that culture, his mantra had become, "It's the numbers, the numbers, the numbers!" This way of thinking had its roots in the idea that businesses are like machines, and that all their aspects, including their employees, need to be managed as mechanical parts. With regard to managing people, what makes this image workable is a mostly unconscious belief that the intelligence and character of human beings is fixed early in life, a product of genetics and environmental conditions. In other words, this approach follows from the premise that people are slaves to their patterns, their roles, and their destinies.

In business, this belief system leads to a desire to utilize employees well and to create the right kind of stimuli, in the form of rewards and punishments, to create motivation. These two characteristics, utilization and motivation, are expressed in a wide range of management systems, from benevolent paternalism to command-and-control authoritarianism. In a benevolent system, managers are taught to find people's strengths and place them in positions where these strengths can flower in ways that benefit the company. In more authoritarian systems, employees are rated by supervisors or peers and slotted into positions based on their ranking. In both cases, the tendency is to create a self-reinforcing feedback loop in which performance is determined by how people are defined.

A belief that people have functional strengths and weaknesses that managers need to work with or work around shows up in all kinds of business practices and programs. If you've ever been subjected to feedback, performance reviews, IQ tests, personality assessments, strength finders, culture surveys, incentive programs, rating and ranking, or recognition programs, then you've been looked at through this lens. In fact, the vast majority of corporate programs are based on this belief system and the machine analogy that lies behind it.

Companies that operate from the mindset that people are basically predictable and that their ability to perform is predetermined by their heritage and history tend to be structured, hierarchical, centralized, and bounded. Their cultures are founded on the functional view of human beings as working parts in an engineered or mechanized system. The role of management is to provide clear guidance, ensuring that people's attention is appropriately directed and the coordinated function of the whole system is maintained. Such companies rely heavily on procedures, job descriptions, written communications, and reporting relationships to maintain clarity and order.

A business that views itself and its employees in primarily utilitarian terms will measure success almost wholly based on performance. It will reward results in the form of increased pay or rank. This is based on what appears to be the intuitively obvious and scientifically proven idea that people can be motivated by self-interest. Unfortunately, motivation by means of incentive programs has a subtly corrosive effect on the company as well as society at large. It plays to people's lowest instincts, encouraging self-aggrandizing behaviors at the expense of others and even at the expense of the overall success of the organization.

Work Design for Human Growth

When Chad Holliday was still a relatively young director of strategic planning for DuPont, we had a lively exchange about what it takes to grow strong managers. This stemmed from a conversation about how to prepare leaders for promotion to executive roles. As we shared ideas, I asked him to talk about his own experience.

He responded, "Well, DuPont has a program that moves its high-potential leaders every two years. Being repeatedly uprooted has been hard on me, as well as on my family, but it really helped me grow the knowledge and perspective that would enable me to understand a complex organization, its diverse functions, and how they fit together."

"What makes the program effective?" I asked him.

"As individuals, we need to be invited out of our comfort zones if we want to grow. We need to be thrown into situations that are unfamiliar, that force us to change perspective. Without having someone hold our feet to the fire, it can be difficult to muster the necessary will."

"Okay, I understand that. But do you have any experience of gaining that knowledge and perspective in some other way?"

"No, not really. College?"

"What if you could grow knowledge and perspective in every person, with regard to every function, and in carrying out every task? What if you could do this on an ongoing basis, without uprooting people, based on their own initiative rather than on challenges imposed externally by the company? What if they invited themselves out of their comfort zones because they were moved by the possibility of making a positive difference in the world?"

"Now you've got me curious!"

We set to work, and within a year Holliday had demonstrated to himself how limited his understanding of human growth had been. His starting point was a basic belief that people have an authentic self that wants to be integrated into every part of their lives—a belief that is both reasonable and a huge improvement on thinking of people as machines. From this perspective, work has to do with helping people express their true natures.

There are four external conditions that need to be present for this personal growth to occur:

- Opportunity
- Autonomy
- Sense of purpose
- Support for the process

People develop new skills and insights when they are challenged, and the role of business is to provide the right kinds of challenges, along with the mentoring, coaching, and training that support success.

This way of thinking grew out of the work of a number of psychologists and social theorists—including Abraham Maslow, Carl Rogers, and Virginia Satir—who were attempting to address a broadly held notion in the mid-twentieth century that work and society had become empty of meaning. They introduced ideas of human growth and development into the workplace as a way to increase employees' sense of self-definition and meaning. They proposed that instead of rewarding and punishing people based on outcomes, employers should reward people on the basis of their effort, perseverance, and risk taking. Their efforts yielded a new, compassionate view of workers as learners, able to be challenged by and grow from their experiences.

Carol Dweck is a Stanford University professor whose research explores how people become motivated to grow. She advocates that business leaders stop focusing narrowly on results and begin to praise people for demonstrating the courage that allows them to move beyond their comfort zones. This approach, which creates a judgment-free environment, reinforces employees' self-confidence and increases their sense of control over their choices.[2] Whereas a purely performance-based business motivates employees based on self-interest, a business that is focused on human growth motivates its people by founding its corporate culture on values such as autonomy, personal development, and sense of belonging.

The need to create opportunity and autonomy for employees has driven such organizations to minimize hierarchies or, in rare instances, to eliminate them altogether. They introduce teams who engage in collaborative decision making with regard to operations. They value the wholeness of people and encourage them to express themselves. Underlying these methods is the concept that a business should pursue continuous improvement in every arena, including not just financial results but also human expression. The most meaningful indicator of success is improvement in all arenas.

It is helpful to remember that the human-growth approach mostly arose as a reaction to an overemphasis on efficiency. Many people intuitively understood that human beings have an inherent tendency to grow and change and would perform at least as well in a humane and open environment as in a strict hierarchy. This intuition has been borne out by plenty of research, which has begun to influence the thinking and practice of many managers and human resource professionals.[3,4] As a result of this popularization, an explosion of new technologies and programs has come out of the academic and consulting worlds.

But there is a hidden downside to these programs. The belief system may have changed, but not the methodology, which continues to drive behavior through the manipulation of external conditions. A human growth approach, superior though it may be to one that is purely performance based, still fails to address the development of the capacity to reflect and manage one's own motivation. Self-managed development—the source not only of true human development but also of inspired and inspiring business—is the new frontier in the evolution of work design. It is also the focus of the systems regeneration approach.

Work Design for Systems Regeneration

A regenerative business is created through an inherently systemic work design that grows the capacity for systemic thinking and action in the entire organization. Human beings create systems in order to manage what would otherwise be a chaotic experience of the world. A system (for example, an economy) creates a pattern within which we can engage in a recurring process (such as economic exchange) toward a particular purpose (in this case, wealth creation). Once we have a system, we can examine its effects and set about improving it. Through our choices and actions, we impact the ability of systems to serve us and carry out their intended purpose.

A business that adopts a systems regeneration approach moves the boundary of what it is taking into account. It begins to take responsibility not only for its own internal systems (such as accounting or production in our economy example) and the systems in which it is immediately embedded (such as markets or distribution networks), but also for the larger social and natural systems that we depend on collectively. By extending its purview in this way, a business is able to become much more strategically powerful within its markets and its industry, and in society at large.

The core belief behind this approach is that the highest source of motivation comes from the longing—buried deep inside every human being— to live a meaningful life: to make a significant contribution to something important. This longing, once awakened, goes far beyond self-expression or self-interest because it is oriented to something larger and more compelling. It leads people into lifelong quests to grow their own capacities and capabilities in service to what seems self-evidently important and necessary. What awakens this deep impulse will be different for different people, but the quality of selfless caring is universal and represents what most of us point to as the highest expression of human life.

A regenerative business matches this capacity for selfless caring to the larger systems that need to be improved in the world. Through the leveraged instruments of collective work and accumulated capital, a business enables its members to be powerfully effective agents for systemic change. It provides them with a platform for engaging in enlightened disruption.

Seventh Generation: Systems Regeneration in Action

Susan Johnson was an excellent saleswoman at Seventh Generation, a small but visionary company where she first experienced the power of work design focused on developmental potential. Seventh Generation had built its reputation around providing sustainable home and personal care products. It focused on eliminating products that were toxic for the environment, replacing them with products whose production and use were benign.

Before I began working with Seventh Generation in the role of business design consultant, the company was pretty happy with its way of managing people and thought of itself as an exemplar of social responsibility. For example, it encouraged self-actualization through extensive participation in teams that worked on everything from business problem solving to employee health to social and environmental responsibility. People largely managed themselves, and the few supervisors served primarily as advisors and coaches. It was, in other words, a good place to work. But at that point, it was growing neither its markets nor its financial performance.

As part of a change process initiated to help Seventh Generation become more successful by becoming a regenerative organization, I helped create a new kind of team, a core team that was responsible for strategy development and execution. Johnson was invited to be a founding member. This team became the focus of my effort to educate the company in a whole new way of thinking. Over time, it initiated changes that transformed the way the business saw itself and how all employees defined their roles. Through ongoing education and development sessions, Johnson became aware that her prior education had emphasized fragments, such as sales quotas and techniques, rather than wholes. Suddenly she understood the world in terms of systems and their interactions.

Johnson and I would sometimes go out to dinner after these sessions, and on one occasion she told me, "I'm finding myself waking up at night. Last time you were here you introduced us to the idea of nested systems, in which I am part of a larger system, which is part of a larger system. I keep thinking about the larger implications with regard to the kind of impact my work has in other people's lives. I never imagined that my choices would affect so many more people than the retailers I was selling to.

"You keep asking us to reflect on our ripple effects, and I've begun to see my retailers' customers and their children and the schools they attend. It's one continuous flow, through which my actions ripple out to touch so many different kinds of people. I realized today that I can't un-know what I know. I am part of nested systems, and I feel determined to use my knowledge to make more intelligent choices. The process of continuous reflection has made these connections vivid to me. Not only do I know that I have to think about nested systems, but I'm beginning to understand how to work within them to help this company create a better world!"

At the next team meeting, Johnson told her colleagues that she had deliberately crafted a promise to serve a particular group of consumers, a *promise beyond ableness* that went far beyond her current level of capability and thrust her into a course of intense personal and professional development. Specifically, she had selected as her focus Seventh Generation's customers for baby care products (disposable diapers, wipes, and lotions), a group referred to within the company as "natural parents." Johnson's motivation came out of a realization that many parents had a fairly narrow view of what was involved in keeping a baby healthy and safe. She felt that the company was uniquely positioned to provide education and support to these parents. This determination was also consistent with the company's explicitly stated intention to serve as "a primary educator about health at the intersection between homes and Earth."

As Johnson reviewed the situation, she came to see that she needed to create an entirely new relationship with the distributors of Seventh Generation baby products. She asked the retailer Babies-R-Us to help her develop ways to carry out her promise. Babies-R-Us staff knew that harried parents were making quick, uninformed purchase decisions, based on price or brand recognition. Such decisions unintentionally contradicted the customers' values because they weren't based on adequate information and education. The challenge was to create a quick intervention that would get shoppers' attention and educate them in the store.

The explicit goal of the program was to invite parents to think beyond products to what was involved in creating healthy environments for their babies. Johnson conceptualized a "community of natural parents" who could access the latest information and communicate with one another about what they were learning. She started to plan a program for Seventh Generation to share information with customers in the store, thus inviting them into the growing learning community. This inherently altruistic program would create long-term benefits for both Seventh Generation and Babies-R-Us by helping them become trusted advisors to parents.

Johnson began to assemble a research library of all the latest information on infants and household toxins. She built an education program for all of the employees at Babies-R-Us, and she established what at the time was a pioneering effort to create an online community. Based on her research, she chose to focus initially on environmental toxins brought unintentionally into the home.

Using her highly developed sales skill, Johnson went on the road and trained staff at every Babies-R-Us store in the United States. She inspired salespeople to discover their own passion for healthy baby environments, and she provided them with coaching cues to initiate brief but educational conversations with customers. For example, salespeople introduced customers to research about the effects of toxins tracked into homes on the bottoms of shoes. Interested customers could follow up by going online to Seventh Generation's website, where this research was posted. As a result of this program, Babies-R-Us developed a strong identity as a store with a highly educated workforce that cared deeply about the welfare of babies and parents.

In addition to educating consumers, the online community also helped educate Seventh Generation about the many nontoxic products consumers were seeking but couldn't find. This led to the development of a complete, well-integrated system of products designed to support healthy babies and families.

When Johnson's program was launched and starting to bear fruit, she told me, "Well, I'm hooked. It's scary to promise to take on something important that you don't know how to do, but it's worth it because it clearly makes a difference for real people. And it's possible for me because I'm part of a team where everyone is stretching in the same way. That creates an amazing environment of mutual support and challenge. I'm already looking at what my next promise will be, and I have to tell you, work has never been so much fun."

The excitement that Johnson conveyed to me was generated by her firsthand experience as a member of a new kind of workforce in a new kind of workplace—a profound departure from business models of the twentieth century. The regenerative organization is based on a twenty-first-century understanding of work design for effective human development.

Making the Business Case for Regenerative Work Design

The emerging business environment of the twenty-first century demands that businesses be nimble, resilient, and—above all—innovative. They will require intelligent and adaptable workforces that are capable of anticipating and responding to evolutions in markets long before they become generally apparent. Without this intelligence and adaptability, more than 60 percent of businesses worldwide are expected to fail within the next two decades.[5]

Not surprisingly, executives are focused on how to build these qualities into their companies. These days, the questions they ask me tend to focus on six current, pressing issues that are the main drivers of change for business at this time. Fortunately, all of these issues can be addressed through a regenerative approach to work design.

1. *How can I hire and retain top talent?* A trend toward increasingly high standards has launched a talent arms race, making it both more difficult and more expensive to find the key people a business needs to thrive. What makes this phenomenon even more exhausting is the belief that businesses need to compete for each and every employee hired, even though the results of this approach have been mixed at best.[6,7]

   A regenerative organization focuses on developing its talent rather than buying it. It builds critical thinking and personal capacity within a culture of systems regeneration. In other words, every member of the organization gets smarter and more innovative with regard to how to transform the lives of its stakeholders, in the same way that Susan Johnson was able to create a community of informed parents and healthier babies. Instead of wasting energy chasing a limited pool of talent, a regenerative organization grows talent in everyone it touches.

2. *How do we become a "best place to work"?* The popular notion of best places to work pressures companies to meet increasingly sophisticated standards for work environments that people love. Even companies that are not striving to be awarded a place on one of the popular lists know that they are being judged by the same standards and feel a need to understand what it takes to qualify.

   A regenerative business never thinks in terms of best place to work because doing so orients its people to be motivated by self-interest. Instead, a truly forward-thinking business sets out to be the best place for its employees to make a contribution to a greater good. The work design, itself, rather than amenities or human resource programs, motivates people to become part of the organization and to take on more and more challenging work because they feel themselves to be part of a future that they want to help create.

3. *How can I make my company an innovation powerhouse?* Companies today are well aware that the capacity to innovate depends on cultural conditions and workforce capabilities that are elusive and difficult to create. They also know that unless they develop this capacity quickly and to a high degree, they will inevitably be out-competed in our rapidly evolving world.

   A regenerative organization sees innovation as the responsibility of everyone, not the province of a specialized team. It moves innovation out of the R&D lab and into every working team. As part of the work design, each individual commits to making an extraordinary contribution and is given the support needed to carry through on that promise. This is a condition of employment. As a result, a regenerative business moves from making incremental improvements in what exists to making radical breakthroughs in brand new territory.

4. *How do we build the resilience to weather wild fluctuation in our markets?* Financial performance comes from the ability to be creative by using the forces at work in both up and down markets. This requires unusual systemic thinking abilities from a workforce.

   For a regenerative business, financial effectiveness comes from effectively managing both top-line growth and bottom-line returns. The aim of regenerative work design is to shift a business's orientation away from selling more of the same product to more new customers to becoming the industry leader in product and service development for a fiercely loyal, reliably growing customer base.

5. *How do we deal with ever-increasing complexity?* Senior executives used to manage complexity on their own by changing goals, incentives, and performance measures in response to changing conditions. Unfortunately, this approach is simply too slow and cumbersome for an increasingly fast-moving world. More and more often, people throughout organizations are expected to make complex decisions, which demands new levels of capability on their part. This is a top concern currently driving the competition for talent acquisition.

   By design, a regenerative business sees through the chaos to the patterns that will allow a system to evolve and designs its work to respond to the opportunities that are revealed. Rather than creating jobs, a regenerative business creates space for reinvention.

6. *How can I make my company a healthy place to work?* Businesses are keenly aware of the impact of health on productivity, profitability, and quality of life for their workers. A number of long-term studies have demonstrated a causal relationship between work design and people's health and sense of well-being.[8,9]

Research shows that people experience health and well-being at work when they have a sense that they are making life better for customers and other stakeholders.[10]

Because a regenerative business has a systems-actualizing orientation, it creates the conditions for workers to innovate with regard to how their work is going to benefit people and systems outside of the business. Thus it guarantees that its workforce will remain healthy.

A regenerative organization enables its people to effectively address the challenges presented by today's world. It sets the stage for people and groups to proactively direct change—in themselves, in the lives of their customers, and in democratic societies as a whole. I have been personally inspired by the realization that building a better business builds a better human being and a better democracy. A regenerative business grows the thinking capabilities and caring capacities of its members. This is precisely how one grows a more capable workforce and citizenry.

CHAPTER THREE

Source Work Design from First Principles

I think it's important to reason from first principles rather than by analogy. The normal way we reason is by analogy—like something else that was done, or what other people are doing. With first principles you [get] down to the most fundamental truths and reason from there.

Elon Musk, Entrepreneur and Inventor

O UR WORLD IS DIMENSIONAL, **whole, alive; and continuously evolv-** ing, but our inherent capacity to understand it in these terms has mostly been trained out of us in favor of analytic methods that dissect, compartmentalize, and lineate. As powerful as these methods can be, they make it almost impossible to think systemically. This is why I believe that it is important to build the development of critical- and systemic-thinking capabilities directly into work design.

This chapter offers criteria for building a business that powerfully supports the development of individuals. Chapter 4 focuses on ways to create an effective and motivated work community. Chapter 5 highlights the multitude of common business practices that must be rooted out if you are to generate any kind of meaningful change for your organization. Taken together, these three chapters provide an overarching blueprint for regenerative work design. When implemented as a coherent system, they build in the qualities that make a regenerative business distinctive.

Three Criteria for Growing Human Capacity

The following three criteria work on growing human capacity by focusing on three fundamental factors that enable people to take the kind of risk that produces strong businesses (and, by extension, strong individuals, families, and democracies). The first, *internal locus of control*, has to do with the degree to which one is able to take full responsibility for one's actions. The second, *external considering*, is the ability to take into account and care deeply about the effect of one's actions on other beings. The third, *personal agency*, is an essential characteristic in individuals who wish to become fearlessly proactive with regard to evolving a system.

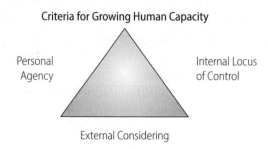

Using these criteria, it is possible to test the regenerative potential of any work design. For a business or any other organization to work in a coherent and systemic way, all three must be present and rigorously cultivated. If they are only partially present or diluted by a mix-and-match assemblage of off-the-shelf programs, then it is impossible to build the force needed to create a great company.

Each is a standard not only for the development of a workforce, but also for the outlook and practice of management, which is responsible for ensuring that the characteristics they measure are continually nurtured. They are built into the work design by making employees responsible for everything from initiating strategic thinking and actions to self-evaluation with regard to performance.

Instead of organizing teams around activities in response to customer surveys and feedback, meeting these criteria requires that teams project themselves into the lives of customers. From this perspective, teams are able to anticipate and address in advance the impacts that changes in markets or governing infrastructures will have on customers. Even more important, they work to understand goals and aspirations that customers are seeking to realize in their lives, yet may not know how to articulate.

The creation of the Google Food Lab offers a good demonstration of the synergy that can occur when a self-starting individual finds herself in a business environment that emphasizes internal locus of control, external considering, and personal agency. When Michelle Hatzis, PhD, left the Kaiser Permanente health care system to join Google, she found herself in a completely new business culture with the authority to dedicate 20 percent of her time to a self-directed project. In conversation with Michiel Bakker, Google's global food director, she identified the need to engage food experts to help develop the Google Food program. At the time, the company's culture didn't allow for advisory boards, and so working together, Hatzis and Bakker came up with the idea of the Google Food Lab.

The particular genius of this idea was that it represented an extension beyond Google's ubiquitous search engine platform. Hatzis led an ongoing series of meetings that brought together leaders, practitioners, and researchers from around the world and across multiple aspects of the industry. Through their conversations, these experts began building a detailed, collective understanding of the intricate complexities of the global food system and its impacts. They then collaborated on research, sharing their results through a broad array of technical and industry journals and events. In this way, Hatzis and the Food Lab network arrived at a new, highly effective way for Google to fulfill its mission of "universally accessible information."

Criterion One: Internal Locus of Control

Locus of control refers to a belief about where power lies with regard to the events in people's lives. *Internal* locus of control arises when people understand that they have full responsibility for their actions, how they experience the world, and the outcomes they produce for themselves and others. *External* locus of control, on the other hand, arises when people believe that success and failure are beyond their control (e.g., the products of luck, genetics, circumstance, or the actions of other people). Abundant research has demonstrated that an experience of internal locus of control is directly correlated with healthy, happy, productive lives, and thus it makes sense for businesses to make it a cornerstone of work design.[1,2,3]

People who consistently develop and exercise internal locus of control practice three core capabilities: *nonattached integrity, inner aims*, and *reflective self-accountability*.

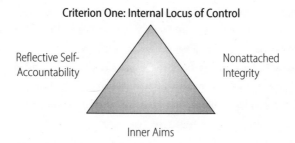

Criterion One: Internal Locus of Control

Reflective Self-Accountability

Nonattached Integrity

Inner Aims

Nonattached Integrity

Integrity relies on clarity about what one believes is true or good, while nonattachment has to do with remaining open to the possibility that these beliefs may evolve as the result of self-examination and engagement with others. In order to remain true to themselves, people must practice continual self-discovery and *nonattached integrity*, but in any organization (and particularly in teams), the social pressure to go along in order to get along can be intense. The effect in a creative venture is loss of full access to people's intelligence and imagination.

What it means to remain in integrity evolves with our self-understanding. This is why cultivating nonattachment to self-image and the impressions of others is so important. Nonattached integrity allows each of us to remain authentic and to contribute a distinctive perspective, even as we engage in collective endeavors.

Inner Aims

Internal locus of control relies on people's ability to remember what inspires and motivates them. Without conscious effort, they fall into old habits and inadvertently violate their intention to be accountable and in integrity. We all need a practice to recall us to ourselves, moment to moment, and remind us of the person we want to be. An *inner aim* is a distilled instruction, a compact and talismanic phrase (like a mantra) that we create to serve this purpose. Some common examples are, "Be present!" "Judge not." "Breathe."

Aims become most powerful when they are uniquely tailored to our inner lives. Unlike affirmations, which are directed toward getting more of what we want out of life, an inner aim calls forth the states of being and capabilities that enable us to contribute to life.

Reflective Self-Accountability

Internal locus of control becomes possible only when people are able to be personally responsible, doing what they say they will do in order to produce what they say they will produce. *Reflective self-accountability* is the practice of noticing when we have fallen short of delivering on a promise and taking action to make it right. This practice energizes and satisfies us precisely because it places control in our own hands and requires that we learn to see ourselves and our behaviors accurately.

Many management practices actually impede the development of internal locus of control. For example, structured feedback invites people to place their attention on what others think rather than develop their own capacity for reflection. This actually weakens their ability to be self-determining and self-correcting with regard to thinking and behavior.[4] Another example is reward and recognition programs, wherein supervisors decide who deserves to be singled out for their accomplishments. These promote the mental habit of looking to others to evaluate success, and they undermine the necessary capacity for internal self-assessment.

It takes a great deal of effort to maintain internal locus of control because so many of our social and educational systems inadvertently undermine the capabilities necessary to practice it. To access the motivational power that this criterion delivers, a business must proactively build it into work design.

Criterion Two: External Considering

External considering, which means caring deeply about something or someone in addition to ourselves, is a concept developed by Armenian philosopher G. I. Gurdjieff as a way to counter the nearly universal human tendency to be narrowly self-referential. Gurdjieff observed that self-reference diminishes the meaning in our lives by preventing us from understanding the unique and creative roles we could be playing in the world. External considering requires understanding that what we care about is whole and alive, with its own purposes and potential, and it demands the reflective capability to understand how our actions contribute to or diminish this potential. Like internal locus of control, external considering requires three core capabilities: *core discernment*, *engaged caring*, and *will to create*.

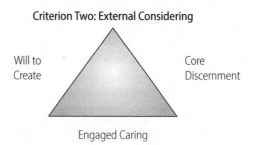

Criterion Two: External Considering

Will to Create

Core Discernment

Engaged Caring

Core Discernment

The act of engaging in external considering requires *core discernment*, seeing through current conditions to the enduring cores and underlying organizing patterns of living beings. This is facilitated by understanding how living systems are nested within one another and the potential that can be expressed through systemic relationships.

For example, anyone who has observed children going through puberty will have noticed them trying a variety of strategies as they attempt to fit into their social environment. They experiment with how to dress and flirt, new ways of speaking, and new sorts of body language. Because these behaviors are all about fitting in, they should not be mistaken for the child's essence or core self. For a parent, teacher, or guardian, the trick is to discern the core of the child behind the behaviors.

Our natural tendency is to experience phenomena primarily through our senses and to accept this information at face value, as though it were a complete description of reality. Recognizing patterns, on the other hand, is a discipline that requires discernment based on critical thinking. It needs to be grown through practice.

Engaged Caring

Engaged caring refers to an active commitment to increase the capacity of others to fulfill their own purposes and potential. This makes it different from qualities that are often confused with it (and often complementary to it). For example, kindness and empathy, which are important for social harmony, allow us to demonstrate a sense of shared humanity. Compassion causes us to want to alleviate suffering. Engaged caring goes further. It honors individuals' responsibility for realizing their own potential, and it recognizes the power, inspiration, and dignity that become accessible to them when they take up this task.

True caring requires compassion, generosity, and selflessness. It involves restraining our self-centered tendencies to provide people with answers or do their work for them. Instead, we keep an eye on the larger selves that they are growing into and dedicate ourselves to helping them build the capabilities that this growth will require. The quality of caring helps us manage our egos so that we can pursue the investments in the futures of others that external considering makes possible.

Will to Create

One of my fundamental beliefs is that people come most alive and feel the greatest meaning in their lives when they can see how their actions create benefit for something beyond themselves. This is their source of *will to create*, and it needs to be at the center of our attention if we want to engage in external considering with regard to others. It requires us to develop the capability in ourselves and others to anticipate and communicate systemic consequences of actions, because understanding how what we do will ripple out into the world lets us know that our work is important and necessary.

Companies are constantly organizing to make things easy for themselves (and for the most part, they are fooling themselves if they believe that customers don't know it). External considering requires something entirely different: that businesses extend their thinking to the real lives of customers and therefore the unexpressed potential within them. In other words, companies must become strategic thinkers on behalf of their customers. I am not talking here about the inane promise to "fulfill customers' needs better than anyone else." When a company and its employees engage in real caring, they go beyond looking at needs and instead focus on what customers could become.

Criterion Three: Personal Agency

Personal agency refers to the strong inner urge that people have to be active players in the world, taking responsibility for manifesting the effects they want to create. Personal agency is important to businesses because they need people who are able to take appropriate initiative. A workforce made up of people who can see what needs to be done and who will step up to do it is far more powerful than a workforce that depends on delegation to know what to do. The three core capabilities that activate personal agency are *nodal realization*, *self-efficacy*, and *promises beyond ableness*.

Criterion Three: Personal Agency

Promises Beyond Ableness

Nodal Realization

Self-Efficacy

Nodal Realization

A node is a point in a system where a relatively small intervention can have a big effect. Realization refers to the ability to envision the dynamics occurring in any system and the effects that will ripple out from a particular intervention. People with insight into how industries and societies work are able to be powerfully effective disruptors in even the most entrenched and dysfunctional systems. This capability is based on *nodal realization*, an understanding of where the nodes in a given system reside and how action at these points of origin can effect change throughout the whole.

Acupuncture offers a way to envision what I mean here. A skilled acupuncturist inserts a needle at a single point to address symptoms throughout a patient's body. In the theory of acupuncture, this is possible because there are specific nodes or locations in the body through which energies flow in multiple directions. Similarly, if businesses want to improve relationships with their customers or motivation in their employees or the overall health of their industry, there are certain nodes where a relatively small intervention can have a big effect. For example, engineers at DuPont upgraded the value of hydrogen peroxide by shifting focus off of what was essentially a commodity and onto the process of paper making. One of peroxide's virtues is that it bleaches without damaging fibers or polluting water. The rapid increase in expertise that this shift made possible caused DuPont to become indispensable to a rapidly evolving paper industry.[5]

Nodes are rarely visible. They have to be discovered by understanding or imagining how a system would work if it were concretely expressing its unique potential. Then we must conceptualize an optimal entry point to crystallize a new pattern. This is not an easy task to accomplish—nodes are not easy to find—which is why most businesses fall back on the shotgun approach to change: "Start anywhere, so long as you start!" But this fallback approach simply results in spending lots of energy without being particularly effective. Making the effort to identify nodes is foundational to developing personal agency, which always starts by finding something focused, systemic, and self-evidently important to work on.

Self-Efficacy

Fundamental to personal agency is *self-efficacy*, the trust that we can figure something out, regardless of how unfamiliar or difficult it may seem. Self-efficacy comes when people understand themselves and the processes that they use to successfully take on new arenas of challenge. The deliberate development of self-efficacy is a powerful antidote to the pervasive passivity and fear of failure found in most organizational cultures.

In businesses, self-efficacy is grown in a deliberate and explicit way by asking employees to find and pursue appropriate challenges for themselves. This request is most effective when it is accompanied by an invitation to engage in structured reflection on the processes they use to rise to the challenges they choose. Together these activities foster holistic learning so that employees are able to become conscious of and develop control over their unique ways of mastering complex situations. As they repeat this process through time, they extend the boundaries of what they are able to take on.

Promises Beyond Ableness

Personal agency is ignited when people rise up to challenges beyond what they imagine is possible. A *promise beyond ableness* requires that people muster the will to work on a system beyond the one in which they usually operate in order to make a vitally important change or contribution to an even larger whole. By definition, it is something that people don't already know how to do, and for this reason it requires a high level of self-efficacy. A promise beyond ableness—like the promise Susan Johnson made at Seventh Generation to create a program for natural parents—is the opposite of under-promising and overdelivering, which comes from a desire to manage the expectations of others. Rather, it embraces the unlimited aspirations people can hold for themselves and the better world that they want to help create.

This does not imply that I am advocating promises *without* ableness: taking shots in the dark and hoping for the best. Promises beyond ableness are rigorously vetted and intended to build on capabilities that people have already developed. They are instruments by which people evolve themselves to take on increasingly significant challenges. An individual's promise beyond ableness is always a collective enterprise because pulling it off requires the support, resources, and wisdom of a community. This is precisely why businesses are fertile ground for instigating systemic disruption—they provide a rich and supportive social environment within which individuals can pledge themselves to produce extraordinary impacts.

Personal agency is a critical component for businesses that want to become disruptive and innovative organizations. Without agency, workers simply wait for instruction or approval to take a next step. In most companies, the work of innovation is delegated to a small group, while everyone else carries out ideas that have been handed down or developed for them. This severely limits available creative energy. The force that lets a business create radical change is released only when *all* of its people are passionately engaged in creating and holding themselves accountable for innovations that will make a difference in the larger world.

The Necessary Connection among These Criteria

I propose that interaction and integration among all three of these criteria—*internal locus of control*, *external considering*, and *personal agency*—is necessary for any profound disruption to occur. When one drops out, the result is usually a shortfall in vision or execution. When there is not enough internal locus of control, for example, the forces of an entrenched status quo can easily overwhelm any change effort, no matter how worthy or inspiring. Anyone who commits to a course of action that fundamentally calls into question the social consensus about what is true and necessary will need to have developed a high degree of grit and integrity.

For a person or a group with high levels of internal locus of control and personal agency, the absence of external considering creates the risk of becoming greedy. This is the origin of the so-called "one percent," who are skilled at accruing wealth for themselves rather than for the benefit of the whole of society. Without adequate development of their external considering, many of the people who could contribute the most to social evolution lose themselves in the far less satisfying pursuit of personal material gain.

Those who have a strong internal locus of control and external considering but inadequate personal agency risk taking on only what they can get their arms around. In other words, they aim too low. This is a common failing among those who are attracted to the social entrepreneur movement. To be a disruptor, people must look for the change that is truly leveraged in terms of transforming a system, rather than those that attempt to address symptoms. In most cases, this means figuring out what no one has been able to figure out and committing to the steepness of the inevitable learning curve. That's why I call it a promise beyond ableness.

Food Inspiration

Arjan de Boer and Hans Steenbergen are two of the founders of the Dutch media and event planning group Shoot My Food. They share a passionate belief that food is a cornerstone for a humane civil culture and a happy life. When they started their work together, they could see that people in the food industry, given the pressures they faced, were prone to losing contact with their original love of food as a means for creative expression. So they invented a business specifically designed to support the inspiration and development of food professionals. Over time, Shoot My Food has grown into a small media empire that annually hosts a variety of popular events and programs.

From the beginning, de Boer and Steenbergen's dedication to inspiration as a way of life led them to experiment with the work design for their company. They wanted to engage in ways of working that sustained the creativity and passion of every member of Shoot My Food and kept them focused on what food professionals needed to reawaken their own inspiration.

Although this was essentially a media company, it drew its employees from the ranks of recent graduates from cooking and hospitality schools. Each of these young people was invited to contribute to the ideation of the group. The plan was that together they would draw from their own experience and their networks of contacts in the industry to generate insights about what was needed and what kinds of projects could address those needs. They would come together as teams to vet and evolve their ideas. As the process took place, the more experienced members were available to offer support and mentoring to help get projects off the ground, but they were careful not to take over and supervise the work of the younger employees.

Everyone rolled up their sleeves to help with events and project launches. Afterward, they sat down together to audit how it had gone in order to generate "tips and tops"—tips for how to make it better and ideas to top their success with an even greater event next time. In other words, the entire business philosophy was organized around how to tap and foster the creativity, inspired energy, and self-accountability of employees as a way to create events and media products that did the same for their audience.

One new employee, twenty-two-year-old Lucas Vlaar, who was two years out of hotel school, noticed that the photography and video work featured in *Food Inspiration* magazine, a Shoot My Food publication, failed to capture the vitality of the people they were highlighting. He realized that this was because the magazine depended on contract photographers who had no real love for their subjects. So he persuaded Shoot My Food to buy professional video equipment and trained himself as a videographer. Then he took on the production of *Food Inspiration* and made it a global, award-winning publication.

Another group member, Susan Koenders, was interested in the high turnover in the European food industry. She identified that graduates of training schools would work a few years, get discouraged, feel disillusioned, and leave the field. They complained that they had become functionaries within corporations, a far remove from the inspiration that had drawn them into this work in the first place.

In response, Koenders started a Food Service Talent Academy that provided a lively and collegial environment for professionals who wished to extend their practice into the whole process of producing inspired food experiences. Their work together in the academy also taught them ways to connect people to one another and to their larger communities.

Two more group members, Bram Kreté and Tim Kievits, decided to create the Generation Food network to help their millennial peers stay connected. They recognized that many young graduates from European hotel, hospitality, and chef schools were struggling with a sense of isolation as they moved into the workforce. Consequently, Kreté and Kievits decided to create an alumni association that would allow food professionals to grow and maintain the camaraderie and emotional connection that they were missing. In addition, the entire network would benefit from shared intelligence about emerging trends and innovations occurring across the industry.

This generation and execution of exciting new ideas is not limited to Shoot My Food's younger members. De Boer and Steenbergen hold the same expectation for themselves. For example, they decided that they wanted to bring businesses in their field together in a "hippie environment," a fun, informal, natural setting away from the pressures of dealing with consumers. Here they could engage with the culture-creating potential of their work. The result, Food Unplugged, is a popular outdoor festival that mixes food professionals from the arenas of scientific research, service, business, and design.

Shoot My Food is consistent in applying internal locus of control, external considering, and personal agency across the entire organization. Within its culture, delegation and job descriptions are unknown concepts. Everyone is expected to care passionately about their industry and its potential, and to work to improve the lives of the food professionals whom they serve. Everyone is expected to take on challenges that are far outside of their experience and capability, continually raising the bar for themselves, the company, and the industry. Everyone needs to be fully accountable for communicating openly and maintaining the integrity of their work. The result is a company that is wildly creative, fun to be around, and a major industry disruptor.

The Next Step—Creating the Right Conditions

Together autonomy and opportunity for initiative are excellent starting points for human development, given how rare they are in the corporate world. They create the basis for self-actualization. But as good as they are, they do not create an adequate basis for systems actualization. In other words, they are insufficient on their own to create true market disruptions. And they are certainly not adequate for the task of generating changes to social, political, and economic systems. Thus they need to be rounded out by design criteria that focus on creating the right conditions for enlightened disruption. That is the subject of chapter 4.

CHAPTER FOUR

Build Innovation into How Work Is Done

It is critical to design a way of working so that innovation is never optional—for anyone. Innovation has to be built into how choices are made and work gets done.

Carol Sanford

MOST ORGANIZATIONS KNOW that to engage in real, disruptive innovation they need great, creative people. They also understand that they must provide the conditions within which these people will flourish. In addition to a vibrant culture, they must design work in such a way that it invites and even compels innovation. Whereas most businesses do this by hiring and nurturing a small group of creative talent, a regenerative organization establishes the conditions that will grow creativity across the entire organization.

The right conditions can radically expand what people consider possible, while nurturing a compelling desire in them to be part of it. In other words, when the conditions are right, personal growth becomes tied to transformational endeavors. It can even be tied to the disruption of existing economic and social systems. This keeps personal growth meaningful and therefore sustainable. A business accomplishes this by fostering a culture that emphasizes rigorous thinking matched with reliable, structured support.

Three design criteria—*initiative activation*, *developmental infrastructure*, and *change accelerator*—focus on these fundamental conditions. When present, they enable everyone to develop the capabilities described in chapter 3. Businesses that foster a culture in which everyone thinks like a CEO completely bypass the current debates about the relative merits of hierarchical versus flat organizations. Thinking and decision making take place in every part of the organization, regardless of its overall formal structure.

The first criterion, *initiative activation*, is intended to foster the ability of every member of an organization to take initiative with regard to building a world-changing business. The second, *developmental infrastructure*, helps integrate individual initiative and organizational direction in order to achieve mutual success. The third, *change accelerator*, involves orchestrating the conscious dialogue that will ensure that enlightened disruption is actually occurring in the market and society as a whole.

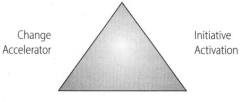

Three Criteria for Growing an Innovation Culture

Change Accelerator

Initiative Activation

Developmental Infrastructure

Human creativity has a tendency to become scattered or diffused without a rigorous discipline in place to focus it. These three criteria are specifically designed to enable businesses to provide focus, organization, and order to the initiatives of their members, so that their creative energy gains coherence and thrust. The criteria also provide guidance for the initiation and management of large-scale change. They are applicable to businesses, communities, ecosystems, and nations because they allow groups to start where they are and grow from there. For this reason, I have found them to be contagious. The minute workers begin to experience and master them within the workplace, they start to carry them out into their communities, where they can be put to use to benefit the public.

In chapter 1, when I described the innovative work of Susan Johnson, a sales director for Seventh Generation who took on the creation of a program for natural parents, I didn't describe the company work design that made it possible for her to do this. In what follows, I draw from my experience with Seventh Generation to illustrate how these three essential criteria play out in a real company.

Criterion One: Initiative Activation

Are people paying attention to what produces evolutionary outcomes, or are they caught up instead in meeting existing, already articulated needs?

Initiative activation is a structured means for drawing out the inherent human tendency for personal agency, bringing it into the business and its endeavors. Most businesses spend people's initiative on proscribed activities that have been delegated by someone higher up in a hierarchy or dictated by the organization's track record. This trains people to be pattern followers rather than pattern generators, and it severely limits the potential for true innovation. Because creative initiative is fundamental to what it means to be fully human, I believe that organizations have a sacred obligation to foster it. It doesn't hurt that highly motivated people who are willing to take initiative are also good for business. *Structured work progression, buyer-focused field teams,* and *responsible financial measures* are factors that create the conditions within which initiative activation can occur in a coherent, strategic way.

Criterion One: Initiative Activation

Responsible Financial Measures

Structured Work Progression

Buyer-Focused Field Teams

Structured Work Progression

In place of the usual climb up the corporate ladder, a regenerative business provides a path of *structured work progression* based on growing capability and scope of endeavor. This requires a set of transparent agreements with regard to what constitutes appropriate work and how it needs to be carried out. When these are in place, all employees are able to self-assess whether the work they initiate justifies the use of organizational resources and supports the overall intentions of the business.

Creative people need something to push against, and in a regenerative business that something comes from a singular, well-conceived and articulated corporate direction, coupled with deep understanding of the buyer groups that this creativity is directed toward. In addition, both people and businesses need escalating challenges that develop the scope and depth of their creativity over time. They need to take on arenas of increasing complexity and initiatives of increasing impact in order to experience themselves continuing to grow.

Buyer-Focused Field Teams

Because a deep understanding of buyers is fundamental to the kind of initiatives undertaken by a regenerative business, it is critical to bring buyer groups to life in the minds and hearts of everyone in the organization. This is done by means of *buyer-focused field teams*, each of which focuses on one key group served by the organization. Every member of the organization sits on one of these teams, which engages in research and deep reflection about the lives and purposes of their chosen buyer group and how to anticipate what would best serve it. Each field team then educates and advocates on behalf of their buyers to the rest of the organization.

Contrast this with the practice of conventional businesses, which delegate thinking about buyers to the marketing and sales team, leaving everyone else to focus narrowly on the standards and procedures by which they carry out their assigned tasks. In a regenerative business, all workers spend some portion of their time each week thinking directly about the effect that their work will have on real people in the world. Because teams are drawn from across the organization, members inevitably cross-pollinate, sharing information with their colleagues about the patterns or gaps they discover in multiple buyer groups. This global intelligence enables individuals to discover initiatives that are strategic and personally inspiring.

Responsible Financial Measures

One reason companies hold tightly to hierarchical structures when it comes to decision making is that every decision has financial implications. Knowledge and understanding of a company's finances are closely guarded by individuals high in the pyramid, and thus so is decision making.

In a regenerative business, where initiatives are launched at all levels of the organization, it becomes critical that every member has a clear grasp of finances and their relationship to overall strategic and ethical imperatives. In particular, workers must understand how cash flow, earnings, and margins are produced and how decisions will affect these key financial measures. Any initiative must be planned in a way that takes fully into account *responsible financial measures* and how these areas will be positively affected without resorting to externalization of social or environmental effects. Every member of the organization is expected to grow this capability and is supported in the effort to do so, which is critical to launching good initiatives and is part of how one builds a company made up entirely of people who think like CEOs.

Initiative Activation at Seventh Generation

Early in my work with Jeffrey Hollender, the founder of Seventh Generation, we agreed to create systems that would enable his people to be self-directing and self-managing and to remove anything that would prevent them from making this shift. Our task was to design a completely different way of operating, but without creating the chaos that ordinarily accompanies radical changes in organizational structure, such as eliminating supervisors or job descriptions overnight.

At the core of this effort, we put in place a progressive work structure designed to evoke an evolving view of how to use personal creativity and initiative to serve the business and its customers. This had the effect of dislodging the habitual notion that a job is a fixed set of tasks and responsibilities handed down from above, usually in the form of a job description. A progressive work structure defined the open space into which all Seventh Generation employees were able to design the contributions they would make.

For this purpose, I offered a matrix that encompassed five key functions of the business, within a hierarchy of complexity and scale of undertaking: managing resources, site, operations, people, and planning. All employees used this matrix to commit to a plan for taking on increasingly demanding challenges within an increasing range of business functions. They typically began with an endeavor that was near the bottom of the matrix, just beyond their current range of capability, and steadily grew the capacity to manage more and more complexity.

The matrix was key to the success of this approach. Rather than a blue-sky process that simply opened up free-form space for people, the matrix set boundaries capable of focusing everyone's creativity. These boundaries came from the strategies and managing principles established by a leadership team drawn from across the company.

In order to develop the concepts with which they would populate the matrix, employees needed to understand what was going on with Seventh Generation's customers. This was the purpose of every employee's participation in at least one of the buyer-focused field teams. Becoming advocates for buyers enabled workers to extend their thinking about what was needed to truly serve their customers. This advocacy translated into innovative ideas for product development, packaging, customer outreach, improved nontoxic formulations, and distribution networks, all of which went onto the matrices of various employees as their promises beyond ableness.

Finally, individual employees ran the numbers and submitted the rationale for their proposal in written form to a team of their colleagues to be tested and challenged. If the proposal successfully got through this gauntlet, demonstrating that it served customers, improved financial performance, and advanced the company's strategy, then the employees were free to start marshalling the resources needed to fulfill their promise.

Criterion Two: Developmental Infrastructure

Is the infrastructure in place that will enable everyone in the organization to build the capacity they need to produce evolutionary outcomes, or are people being trained and mentored to produce only generic results?

Businesses can create a *developmental infrastructure* that enables the establishment and evolution of a regenerative culture by setting up a pattern of recurring processes to support the individual and collective development of all workers. Most organizations seek to achieve this through training, goal setting, and assessment programs, such as culture surveys, performance reviews, and management by objectives. But these programs treat employees generically—as though they are essentially interchangeable—and set about drumming into them what are considered to be the desirable characteristics.

The key to working developmentally is to recognize that all members of an organization are unique. If their creative energies are to be effectively unleashed, then businesses must ensure that this uniqueness is drawn out, realized, and amplified. In other words, a regenerative business engages in external considering with regard to its members, just as it expects them to engage in it with regard to one another, their customers, and the world they are part of. Three factors that enable a business to create this kind of developmental infrastructure include *regular developmental events*, *self-directed work plans*, and *resource roles*.

Criterion Two: Developmental Infrastructure

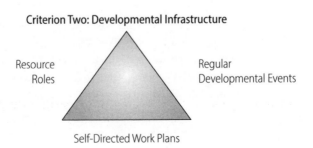

Resource Roles

Regular Developmental Events

Self-Directed Work Plans

Regular Developmental Events

Learning and change occur most effectively through a pattern of recurring, *regular developmental events*, such as in-depth courses in personal and professional development, rather than one-time, concentrated interventions such as retreats or trainings. This is because people need time to test, evolve, and integrate new ideas so that they can begin to use them generatively. Out of this active process of testing and refining they become able to engage the next level of idea, and the next, and the next. Increasingly, they are able to manage their own idea generation through development of the capacity to observe and direct thought itself. They also learn resilience, agility, and caring in the face of a dynamic, complex, and destabilizing world.

This kind of learning unfolds through time and requires learners to be consciously aware of the changes occurring in their mentation and practice. The capacity for this idea generation is innate in everyone, not just in highly educated members of upper-level management. The inclusion of regular developmental events for all employees enables a company to become flexible, intelligent, comprehensive in what it can track and anticipate, and thus disruptive.

Self-Directed Work Plans

In a regenerative business, individuals create *self-directed work plans* for their own development. That is, they design paths for themselves that address the effects they choose to initiate in larger systems, the ways this will strengthen their company, and the kind of personal development that will be required of them.

Unlike the typical approach of companies that are organized from the top down, where work plans tend to be dictated by supervisors based on directives moving down through the hierarchy, this process is both self-directed and collegial. Workers organize their development based on the promises beyond ableness that they make, consistent with the overall strategy of the company and supported by their field teams. They manage the periodic audits and reviews of their progress, and they use regular developmental events to upgrade and evolve their approaches and aims.

By placing so much authority and responsibility directly into the hands of workers and by inviting them to identify goals that are deeply meaningful to them, a regenerative business cuts through many of the barriers to improved productivity. Rather than under-promising so that they can meet their commitments, which is the norm in a hierarchical company, workers organize themselves to improve productivity. Their energy is freed up to work on their own deeply meaningful promises.

Communication problems also begin to disappear when work plans are self-directed because the need for instruction to pass through supervisors is eliminated. When work is self-initiated, workers take responsibility for getting the information they need to succeed. Internal politics also evaporate as internal locus of control becomes established in the business culture. The need to gossip or jockey for position becomes almost irrelevant in an organization without hierarchies or oppressive systems of control.

Resource Roles

A regenerative business replaces the role of supervisor with the entirely different role of functional or developmental resource. That is, people in the company with a high degree of knowledge, skill, and experience in a particular field (such as engineering or marketing) make those capabilities explicitly available to others in service to their promises beyond ableness. People in *resource roles* make their own promises to figure out how to ensure the success of the individuals and teams that they are called on to support.

In addition, a specialized group of *developmental resources* work with employees to grow their overall strategic thinking and self-management capabilities. This represents a natural, evolutionary path for those who had been supervisors in the past, within which their valuable skills are directed to new, truly developmental purposes. The role of a resource is not to engage in performance or pay review, but to focus single-mindedly on whatever will help individuals realize their promises. This aspect of the developmental infrastructure provides a framework for courageous experimentation and risk taking that enables employees to rapidly and successfully extend into innovative territory.

Developmental Infrastructure at Seventh Generation

During the years I worked with Seventh Generation, we put in place a comprehensive program focused on developing all employees' capability to enact the ambitious strategic initiatives they were coming up with. Because of the work we were doing, the company was growing 45 to 65 percent each year in revenues from the successful expansion of its market.[1,2] It needed the intellectual and emotional capacity to handle and get out ahead of this process of near constant growth.

Too often, organizations like Seventh Generation indulge in wishful thinking when it comes to opening up opportunities and setting employees loose to pursue them. They fail to take into account the structure and support that most people need to discover and pursue their own creative potential. This can lead to sink-or-swim situations, where employees who have already developed self-managing capability (through their upbringing or life experience) will succeed and the rest will fall short. By all means, organizations should open up space for employee creativity, but they must also be sure to provide the developmental infrastructure needed for everyone to succeed.

One aspect of this infrastructure is regular exposure to new ideas and ways of thinking. It's a little like going to college, which is a life-changing experience for most people. A college provides structure and progressive learning opportunities, an environment rich with other learners and mentors, and a culture that supports the development of whole, mature, and well-educated individuals who are able to become fully contributing members of society. There is no reason a business organization can't provide the same resources, and in fact, that is the best way to create an unstoppable business.

Seventh Generation developed a very exciting learning environment. Given the fast-moving pace at which the company was growing, the systemic capabilities we introduced were put into practice overnight. We met for several days each month to work on leadership development, strategic planning, and personal development. These sessions then informed the work of the buyer-focused field teams and the project teams. In addition, I worked with a select group who wanted to serve as resources to their colleagues as they sought to implement their individual and team initiatives.

To anchor this work, all employees generated a comprehensive plan for self-management by writing the answers to a structured series of questions that addressed every aspect of their work life. For example, the questions addressed:

- Ways to improve and evolve their ability to carry out work responsibilities
- Their promise beyond ableness and how it would serve to focus their growth
- Specific results they were aiming to achieve from pursuing their promise
- Personal development that would be required to fulfill it
- Resources they could turn to for help with their personal development
- Resources they would rely on to help them fulfill their promise
- Ways they would assess their progress and success

To carry out these plans, they had access to a variety of support systems. The culture of the company was developmental, which meant that everyone was growing their own consciousness and capability. It was natural for them to reach out to colleagues, either individually or in work teams or the field, and to expect their colleagues to help improve their thinking. A special program had been put in place to train a small group of resources who were available whenever an employee needed a thinking partner.

On one occasion, Jeffrey Hollender came to me for help about a core global imperative we had identified in our initial work together: "A working democracy requires an educated citizenry capable of independent thinking." Out of this, the leadership team had established the managing principle: "In every action, every day, work on developing yourself and others." Jeffrey was concerned that people were failing to act on this principle, and he wanted to know what to do about it.

"Well," I responded, "if you want to get people to pay attention to something, you have to create a culture that gives it status and provides ritualized reminders."

He came up with the ritual of going around the business each morning, asking people to give him a report on how they had helped themselves or someone else to grow in the prior day. If they reported that they hadn't, he referred them to a resource for help figuring out how they could become more developmental in their interactions with colleagues. By placing importance on this principle and making it alive day after day, Jeffrey made it a hallmark of Seventh Generation culture.

Criterion Three: Change Accelerator

Does this business self-evidently produce profound and beneficial change in the world, or are its people only working on incremental improvements?

Most businesses work only on internal changes that have to do with how they operate. They try to redirect people's attention and energy through incentives, and those who receive rewards for adopting new behaviors become role models for the rest. Unfortunately, because this kind of program is imposed on people, it destroys motivation, innovation, and personal agency. It's not good for helping people self-manage their existing responsibilities, let alone participate in a change effort. What's needed instead is a *change accelerator*: an approach to change that connects people's motivations to the meaningful effects they could have in the world.

From a regenerative perspective, it's not that people dislike change or don't want to change; it's that they usually don't see a compelling reason to change. A business that sets paltry aims for itself will naturally encounter inertia and resistance. But a business that wants to set the world on fire will set its people on fire, too. A business that wants to be out in front of change, rather than always playing catch-up, will address itself to *evolutionary strategies*, *significance evaluation*, and *generative parameters*.

Criterion Three: Change Accelerator

Generative Parameters

Evolutionary Strategies

Significance Evaluation

Evolutionary Strategies

Through the promises beyond ableness developed by its members, a regenerative organization pursues *evolutionary strategies* on behalf of whole systems—customers, communities, ecosystems, suppliers, and the many living entities with which it engages. Rather than focus on current conditions, it works to enable these communities to manifest what they have the potential to become. In other words, a regenerative business serves as a strategist and research-and-development partner for its stakeholders. This is very different approach from the strategies developed by most businesses, which tend to be self-serving and focused on how to gain a competitive advantage with regard to the position they hold or are trying to achieve within their industry. No wonder customers so often feel ignored by the companies they depend on.

The key for a business to become a disruptor is to see the systems and the people it serves in terms of their evolutionary potential. This is the only way to introduce ideas that are simultaneously beyond what anyone else is thinking, while completely in harmony with the aspirations of customers and other stakeholders. A company that is filled with people who are able to see in terms of evolutionary potential can direct its research and development efforts to meeting stakeholders where they are going rather than where they currently are. In this way it becomes strategically necessary to its stakeholders because its strategies are developed around them.

Significance Evaluation

As evolutionary strategies are developed, an organization that aims to be an industry disruptor will submit them to rigorous testing. For example, Google is famous for pushing its engineers and scientists to ask themselves, "How can this idea be refined so that it generates beneficial effects for all of our stakeholders? Can the effect we are trying to produce be amplified, so that it creates *10x* improvements over what currently exists? How can we design our approach more elegantly, so that it uses fewer resources, less energy, and less effort?" Through this process of *significance evaluation*, what may have started out as a very good idea can become an industry-changing breakthrough. At the same time, the rigorous vetting and upgrading of ideas improves the systemic thinking capabilities of everyone involved.

Usually, companies test the significance of an idea department by department, in purely functional terms. Financial analysts assess whether it works financially, while operations people test whether it fits within the supply chain. This fragmented approach impedes the ability of a company to think holistically and thus generates piecemeal ideas and actions. In a regenerative organization, the starting point for assessing an idea's significance is the effect it will create in the market. This provides an overarching frame of reference, which, along with shared assessment instruments, allows people across the company to integrate their different perspectives and responsibilities within a strategically powerful pursuit.

Generative Parameters

Like individuals, regenerative organizations also define corporate promises beyond ableness for themselves. This is one purpose of strategic planning. When these promises are translated into *generative parameters*, they guide creation of the focus and boundaries within which creatively disruptive work can occur. Focused attention is brought to the arenas within which work needs to be done and the boundaries that need to be met and crossed if the corporate promise is ever to be fulfilled. This reveals the concrete challenges that can awaken will and creativity in individuals and teams. Through a shared focus on the organization's direction and strategy, everyone becomes able to assess the significance and strategic relevance of proposed ideas and projects.

By contrast with the top-down cascade of decision making that is common in business organizations, a regenerative approach defines the playing board and invites everyone to bring their creative intelligence to the game. This is not the same thing as inviting loose cannons to create whatever they want (a common problem when organizations attempt the shift to a flatter, more democratic structure). Rather, people's generative energies are focused by a shared understanding of the audacity of the collective promise beyond ableness and the strategic arenas within which it needs to be pursued. This directs the energies of individuals and teams so that they have a real chance of creating thrust for a company and receiving all of the support and resources they will need to make their ideas a reality.

Change Accelerator at Seventh Generation

From the very beginning, Jeffrey Hollender was clear that Seventh Generation was a platform for creating social change. He wanted to influence the world of consumer products and its impact on ecosystems by running a successful, disruptive business. He also wanted to upend ideas of ownership and capital. And he passionately longed to nourish more vigorous democratic institutions. So the idea of making corporate promises beyond ableness felt natural to the people who were attracted to work at his company.

Seventh Generation made a wholehearted commitment to becoming the R&D and strategic partners of their customers with regard to human and ecological health. They helped invent the market for nontoxic products and pushed their suppliers to develop formulas that would serve it. As their thinking became more sophisticated, they began to discern more differentiated groups for whom their research was important, including babies, pets, people with chemical sensitivities, and professional janitors.

The company was getting very good at developing excellent products, but it was so small that its impact on larger systems remained relatively insignificant, a fact of which Hollender was well aware. When he was invited by Lee Scott, the CEO of Walmart, to speak to his senior leadership team, Hollender knew that he had to set aside his strong biases against the company and craft a message that could land. So he proposed that Walmart make an enormous beneficial impact in the world by addressing two key issues: it should implement a program to require suppliers to reduce packaging, and it should insist on transparency with regard to listing ingredients on labels. Scott and his team decided to pursue these suggestions, and over time the change was felt around the world—a far greater than *10x* impact.

At about the same time, Seventh Generation realized that if it wanted to create more enduring and large-scale changes affecting the health of people and ecosystems, it needed to work on policy at both the local and national scale. So it cofounded the American Sustainable Business Council (ASBC), an organization for like-minded businesses, nonprofits, and policy makers. A high-minded David among corporate-lobbying Goliaths, the ASBC has earned a reputation as a reliable source for sustainability policy, gaining influence in the Obama administration as well as in state and local governments. One of the significant byproducts of this ambitious promise beyond ableness was an awakening among Seventh Generation employees, who became fired up by the courage they saw demonstrated by their company. They began to elevate their own promises, in a few cases going so far as to successfully run for public office.

The Necessary Connection among These Criteria

A regenerative approach to business offers a coherent alternative to the way corporations usually create the conditions to successfully engage in collective work. Hierarchies are successful because they enable everyone to know their role within the system, the work they are responsible for, the group they belong to, resources they can turn to for support, and the measures that will indicate their success.

A regenerative organization provides for the same needs, but in a way that simultaneously addresses the human hunger for development and participation. It provides structures, systems, and processes that are profoundly different from those of a conventional organization but every bit as coherent. These organizing elements are designed to develop the individual creative capabilities of all members of the organization, while at the same time improving business performance and growing stronger citizens.

Taken together, the three design criteria featured in this chapter, supported by those described in chapter 3, will create the conditions for enlightened disruption. They represent a series of increasingly comprehensive interactions through which human initiative is drawn out and evolved in terms of its intelligence and potency.

The coherent application of all six criteria has the effect of awakening entrepreneurial energy across an organization. *Initiative integration* embeds this energy into a collective enterprise, bringing order to it and enabling it to access the resources and support it needs to advance the organization's overall strategic direction. In the process, people are able to advance themselves from one level of challenge to the next, initiating projects of increasing complexity, scope, and significance.

This means that people are using their experience to grow themselves organically and opportunistically. By introducing *developmental infrastructure*, an organization enables people to escalate their growth through processes that develop their critical thinking. It also enables them to participate in developing the organization as a whole by growing a shared, systemic language of innovation that allows collaboration across all levels and functions. This shared language provides the organizing framework that enables cross-disciplinary teams to move with lightning speed to design and implement powerful new programs and projects.

One more dimension is required if an organization aspires to be powerfully disruptive. It needs to focus attention on the places where existing industries, markets, and social systems are failing to live up to their potential. It has to move itself beyond what exists into the world of becoming, and this is why it needs to develop itself as a *change accelerator*. It must reach for the moon, aspiring to make changes that aren't easy, that require everyone's participation, and that spark the dream of what this company could contribute.

But here's the bad news. These conditions can't just be piled onto an existing organization. There are a number of very common and very toxic conditions and practices that need to be replaced as a company moves toward regeneration. This is the subject of the chapter 5.

CHAPTER FIVE

Eliminate Thirty Toxic Business Practices

You never change things by fighting the existing reality. To change something, build a new model that makes the existing model obsolete.

R. Buckminster Fuller, *Critical Path*

A S WE MOVE through different stages of our lives, we are shaped (often unconsciously) by our family and social environments, our cultures, and the character of our times. These social forces frame how we interpret our experiences, and they also affect the decisions and choices we make. Through continual reinforcement, these influences come to seem normal, natural, even inherent and necessary. Unless we expend real effort—such as through personal development or therapy—we can be completely blind to the impact of social forces and the habitual patterns of thinking and behavior they reinforce.

The patterns we develop in response to social forces deposit like layers of sediment in the psyche, and they can significantly constrain our potential. At times, they can even be harmful. For instance, we might have internalized negative messages from our family or school about our worth, beauty, lovability, or intelligence that inhibit our pursuit of fulfilling lives. We also build up layers of patterns arising from different periods in our lives or from different social contexts, and these can be in conflict with one another, causing us to appear self-contradictory. For instance, a girl might receive messages from her community about the importance of becoming a nurturing mother, while receiving messages from her parents about the importance of being independent and professionally successful. As she attempts to reconcile these apparent inner contradictions, she may have no conscious awareness that they arose outside of herself and could possibly have nothing to do with her own unique path in life.

Businesses are just as susceptible to this accretion of unconscious influences handed down from one era and generation to the next. This can cause them to appear self-contradictory or two-faced, for example with regard to how they behave toward employees. Thus, a business can be its own worst enemy when it comes to evolving its capacity to innovate or even to perform effectively.

In order to become regenerative, it's not enough for a business to add a new set of assumptions on top of the built-up layers of old. Instead, the organization must engage in a process of self-examination in order to recognize and root out self-destructive practices that might otherwise prevent the company from pursuing its potential. In what follows, I've collected thirty common business practices that I believe are toxic, and I've identified the likely sources from which they arose. In order to move forward, companies must take deliberate steps to eradicate these practices and replace them instead with the regenerative business practices I will discuss in chapters 6–11.

The Aristocracy Paradigm

Control over ownership leads to bureaucratization

Probably the oldest unconscious belief influencing business practice is the idea that some small segment of the population is superior to the rest and should be entrusted with decision making on behalf of everyone. Personal will, in other words, is replaced by or subordinated to the will of a leader. This idea is reflected in the traditions surrounding kings, organized religions, and ownership of land and other resources as they have been passed down over the past six thousand years. How we articulate what makes someone superior has changed over millennia, at times privileging warcraft, cunning, wisdom, spiritual attainment, inheritance, wealth, or popular acclaim.

This paradigm is still very much alive in many modern institutions, especially business, where the CEO is assumed to be somehow inherently superior and treated accordingly. In work design, it shows up in some of the most ubiquitous, seemingly commonsensical, and unquestioned business practices.

In the business world, control over ownership inevitably results in bureaucracy. Generally, hierarchies refer to structured sets of relationships that rank people or things in levels, one above another. In some cases, hierarchies can be a useful way to make sense of complexity because they allow us to conceptualize different orders of relationship. For example, living organisms are classified into species, genera, and families as a way of indicating how closely related they are.

The problem arises when we habitually use hierarchies not as a way to organize thinking but as a way to organize people to do different levels of thinking. This has led to hierarchical organizations, where ranking is translated into defined levels of authority, responsibility, and power. In most hierarchical businesses, small groups are designated to do significant parts of the creative thinking and decision making on behalf of all the others, profoundly proscribing the contributions that those others are allowed to make. This direct violation of the principles of internal locus of control and personal agency has the effect of undermining intrinsic motivation and accountability.

Delegation flows from hierarchy, as an upper level of authority dictates actions and responsibilities for lower levels. Skillful delegation is highly prized and generally seen as an indication of executive accomplishment. But delegation is inherently fragmenting. It bounds off tasks to be handed down to subordinates, who may never have access to the larger picture that provides the rationale and meaning for those tasks. Also, it means that the decision about which task is important or necessary is always made by the superior, which turns subordinates into functionaries rather than free, creative agents.

Management by objective is a modification of the idea of delegation, which requires people at lower levels of a hierarchy to define what they will accomplish within the overarching goals set by those at higher levels. This is intended to blunt the sting of subordination and designed to allow some measure of autonomy and decision-making authority. However, the boundaries within which individuals can act are still dictated from the top down, and their actions are expected to aggregate into the accomplishment of goals at the levels above them.

Downsizing in a hierarchy is undertaken by top management as a way to preserve the core of an organization (which, not coincidentally, is generally defined as the top management) so that it can live on to fight another day. Such a decision flows down through the hierarchy, usually generating devastating impacts on employees, their families, and their communities. The assumption that the wisdom needed to make such a decision rests at the top cuts a business off from the wisdom of the whole. It also means that the systemic effects of downsizing are externalized and inadequately accounted for.

Businesses harm themselves, their employees, their communities, and their customers when they behave as though market cycles are unexpected, unpredictable, and impossible to prepare for adequately. By not thinking creatively and building agreement across the organization about how it will manage these kinds of uncertainties, businesses miss the opportunity offered by changing circumstances to improve the well-being of employees and stakeholders. As a result, what should be a welcome source of evolution leaves only chaos in its wake.

Job descriptions communicate the place that individuals will fill within the system as a whole and the boundaries within which they may exercise creativity. Job descriptions enable an organization to ensure that all necessary work has been assigned. They are intended to eliminate confusion and conflict about what is expected and what is appropriate. In a hierarchy, job descriptions are always determined by the organization, and the expectation is that employees will adapt themselves to the needs that have been defined.

Job descriptions are particularly corrosive to initiative, personal agency, and innovation. They are based on fixed ideas about the tasks and competencies that a company will need. They fail to take into account that human beings have the inherent ability to observe a changing world, recognize what's going to be needed, figure out how to do it, and learn the skills to produce it. Innovative businesses organize themselves around the intrinsic motivation and creative energy of individuals.

The Machine Paradigm

Control over process leads to routinization

Sometime around the Renaissance, improvements in the technology of clocks led to the metaphor of the universe as a cosmic clockwork or machine. This shift in paradigm enabled the rise of the industrial revolution, which not only celebrated and elaborated the place of machines in the world, but also organized military and social systems (including businesses) to operate like machines. By allowing people to function as interchangeable parts in machine-like systems, the industrial era severed the bondage to particular lords and lands, allowing unprecedented social mobility. But it also dehumanized people by imagining them as generic, interchangeable cogs.

This paradigm is still alive and well in modern business organizations. Its hallmark is standardization: machines depend on reliably identical parts, inputs, and outputs. This has reinforced the use of ideals as benchmarks against which people and work are judged: the closer to the ideal, the more reliably identical something can be. Thus, work design that is informed by a mechanistic perspective will strive to achieve procedural uniformity and standardization.

Typically, a business based on the machine paradigm sees people as skill sets, views tasks as problems to be solved, and treats organization as the means by which people manage the parts to get the results they want. This leads to a host of business practices that have been around so long and are so familiar that they have come to be seen as business realities rather than business choices.

Core competencies are those functional capabilities that need to be present in order for an organization to operate successfully. They are definable and measurable, which makes it possible to assess whether or not they are present. For example, many organizations assess potential recruits based on how proficient they are in currently popular software programs. Functional capabilities are also impersonal, which is key to making personnel interchangeable. A business that requires a core competency can buy it or train for it because the competency is what matters, not a particular individual.

The idea of core competencies is antithetical to innovation. It locks a business into skills that are generic and repeatable. In other words, core competencies are appropriate to situations that are unchanging, rather than to those that are dynamic. They also treat people as though they, too, were generic, rather than unique, creative beings with the ability to learn, grow, and bring something unexpected and inspired to their work.

Recruitment is an extension of the practice of thinking about people in terms of their core competencies. Companies search and hire the competencies they need, either plugging holes in the workforce or bringing in new skills that will be needed in order to extend into new markets or arenas.

This leads the vast majority of businesses to misunderstand and underutilize their most valuable asset—the human drive and intelligence of the people they currently employ. Too many organizations start from the false premise that talent and intelligence are basically fixed at birth: if people haven't developed skills in one arena or another by the time they come to work for the organization, then they probably can't develop them at all. This false belief that talent must be hired because it can't be grown can become a very expensive proposition. In my experience, nothing could be more untrue.

In the past forty years, companies I work with have shown time and time again that the best way to get the talent and innovation a business needs is to grow it in house. When organizations help workers get connected to the aspirations of their customers, there is no ceiling to the challenges the employees can successfully face and the limitations they can effectively overcome. Businesses don't need to be located in centers of enterprise like Silicon Valley or Austin, Texas, in order to be successful innovators. They just need to learn how to develop their people. In the process, they also help make the communities where they are located become more enterprising.

Feedback is a metaphor explicitly derived from machines and introduced into common parlance by early thinkers in the field of cybernetics, or artificial intelligence. It refers to the governing mechanism that notices when a machine is producing too much of something and causes it to scale back or shut down (for example, the thermostat on a furnace that regulates heat).

Although feedback can be remarkably useful in mechanical systems, it turns out to be a very poor metaphor when applied to human beings. Giving people information that shuts them down is actually a bad idea. First, the vast majority of feedback that people offer one another is projection—90 percent, according to a recent article in *Psychology Today*.[1] The deficiency that one person attributes to another is actually far more likely to be their own. By encouraging projection, feedback not only erodes internal locus of control in the person being critiqued, it also undermines integrity and the potential for personal growth in the one doing the critiquing.

Second, the use of feedback in organizations undermines self-management and motivation. Rather than cultivating the capacity to be self-reflective and self-correcting, feedback makes employees increasingly dependent on outside input for knowing how well they are performing. And third, one of the insidious side effects of feedback is conformity of opinion, the tendency of people to become increasingly unwilling to share unpopular perspectives for fear of being chastised or ostracized. This robs a business of the multiplicity of viewpoints that are critically necessary for understanding a complex world.

People and organizations are often willing to tolerate these downsides because of the common belief that feedback is the only way we can gain other people's insights into our own blind spots. But these insights, colored by projection and barbed by annoyance, can very easily have the effect of shutting us down. It's far more useful, and far more accurate, to practice self-reflection as a way to identify for ourselves the key restraints we will need to work on if we are to have the beneficial impact we seek to create in the world.

Problem solving looks at the world in terms of shortfalls with regard to ideals or expectations. This creates cognitive gaps that we feel driven to close, launching a logical and culturally accepted process for seeking solutions. Typically, we make a thorough examination of the problem, generally by breaking it into its component parts and seeking its root material causes. By discovering and eliminating these causes, we expect to address and resolve the problem. This powerful and useful idea emerged from the scientific method and found wide acceptance in the age of industry. However, it places subtle blinders on our thinking and creativity.

Many people believe that problem solving is the source of innovation. However, problem solving is by definition focused on addressing what exists and attempting to make it better. True innovation comes from reaching for the potential in something: its possible manifestations that don't yet exist. Bringing entirely new things into existence is what makes innovation so disruptive, and this is precisely what gets shut down when thinking is defined or circumscribed by problems.

Brainstorming is a method that was developed to address one of the shortcomings of problem solving. Because problem solving is based in existence and relies on evidence, it can reinforce pessimism and critique, making it difficult to get teams to think flexibly and inclusively. Brainstorming was intended as a way to break down inhibitions against putting bad ideas on the table. The theory posited that by creating a nonjudgmental space in which the mind was free to roam, it was possible to generate new thinking.

The problem is that undisciplined thinking such as brainstorming tends to generate undisciplined ideas, usually in the form of long and not especially useful lists. Although brainstorming has been linked to the evidence-based worldview of materialist science, no scientific evidence exists to demonstrate that brainstorming actually works. In fact, the practice of brainstorming contradicts what most of the research into creativity has shown to be true. Creativity requires the discipline of cognitive dissonance—the simultaneous holding in the mind of two apparently contradictory ideas—to achieve breakthroughs.[2,3] This is why Steve Jobs famously disallowed brainstorming, insisting instead on collectively generated images of the lived experience of customers as the basis for design.[4]

Standards and procedures are precise descriptions of the ways that people are meant to do work so that it can be consistent in both execution and outcome. This is critical to the functioning of a social enterprise that has been conceived as a machine. For all parts to work together smoothly, their timing and results need to be highly predictable.

Standards and procedures are among the most forceful means by which independent human beings are translated into cogs. Standards are nearly ubiquitous and often exist across entire industries. They are established by a small group to govern the actions of the many. For this reason, their comprehensiveness and sophistication are limited by the intelligence and experience of their creators. They explicitly restrict the exercise of consciousness, reflection, adaptability, innovation, caring, will, and self-determination. Standards and procedures arise from the fear of variation. Businesses that base their design on this fear preclude the possibility of authentic responses to a living world. Fear is no basis for enlightened disruption.

Binary evaluation is a formulaic process for determining whether actions or investments are achieving their intended purposes. As an extension of the machine paradigm, binary evaluation assesses actions in terms of on or off, white or black. Did we succeed or fail? What do customers like or dislike about our product? Of course, this kind of evaluation doesn't have to be strictly binary. For example, think of the many times you've been asked to rate customer service you've received on a scale of 1 to 5. Still, the basic premise is the same: there are a limited number of options, and the phenomena can be made to fit somewhere within them.

Binary evaluation replaces the inherent complexity of reality with an oversimplified set of choices. Not only does this reduce its effectiveness at giving us a picture of reality, it also reinforces anti-innovative patterns of thought. A binary or multiple-choice set of options creates a frame within which only a very limited number of things are possible. Moreover, it locks us into looking at and evaluating what already exists, thus preventing us from seeing potential in whatever is emerging through time. By way of example, think about the difference between asking, "What did and didn't work?" and "What has evolved since the last time we undertook this action? What's next in its evolution?"

Another characteristic of binary evaluation is that it is usually undertaken by an outside, objective agent (an expert or a customer) with the necessary expertise to assign value. This makes sense because machines are not able to evaluate themselves. Humans, on the other hand, are more than capable of assessing the value of their actions and choices, and this assessment is the source of their creativity and their motivation to improve. When evaluation is externalized, it undermines this motivation.

Metrics-based auditing enables companies to account for the results of each of their actions so that they can know whether they are meeting the standards that they have set for themselves. Metrics were introduced into industry as a way to make processes transparent, objective, and therefore fair. If every worker is expected to produce the same output to the same standards within the same amount of time, then performance can be assessed in objective, numerical terms, and decisions to hire or fire become evidence-based.

Auditing is different from evaluating. Evaluating is focused on whether actions have achieved their intended purpose, while auditing is interested in whether an action has produced its expected, quantifiable output. It is possible to meet all of the numerical benchmarks while completely failing to achieve the purpose. For example, a company can become more and more efficient at producing a less than successful product, while missing the major attributes that its market is looking for, thus losing out on the chance to introduce a successful product instead.

Metrics can be double-edged and need to be used with care. According to a well-known adage, "What you measure is what you get." That is, once a metric has been established, workers will refocus their efforts in order to meet it, regardless of whether that is the most appropriate place to put their attention. In education, this is known as "teaching to the test." In work design and education alike, it can have a seriously debilitating effect, as participants lose touch with the meaning of their efforts in favor of the immediate achievement of the numerical benchmark. This, of course, works in complete opposition to the cultivation of an innovative workforce.

Function teams extend and elaborate the mechanistic approach to work design, making it more flexible and intelligent. Function teams can generate a more comprehensive view of work flow than their individual members can, and in more forward-looking companies they are given responsibility for finding ways to improve work flow. These teams enable redundancy as workers learn to do one another's jobs within a particular segment of the company and can step in as needed to assist or substitute for one another. Such teams can also be assembled to respond to special needs or projects, bringing together different disciplines in an inclusive process with results that benefit from combining the intelligence of members.

The problem is that function teams perpetuate the fragmented outlook that is characteristic of the machine paradigm. They focus on streamlining the inner working of an organization, rather than on discovering what will be required to improve the lives of customers. Through this inward focus, they limit the possibilities for development in both their members and their organizations as a whole. By their very success, they diminish a business's vitality, viability, and potential for evolution.

Restructuring refers to changing the way reporting relationships are organized. For most organizations, restructuring is the preferred method for addressing issues or attempting to create change. It is based on the premise that any problems a company might be facing can be addressed by putting the right people in the right positions and getting various kinds of work under the right umbrellas. For example, a company might change its structure from one that sorts all of its functions into different silos to one that brings together multiple functions around a regional focus.

What most companies miss is that changes in structure, no matter how big or dramatic, will not change the thinking processes of workers. As long as the collective orientation of an organization is internal, fragmented, and functional, restructuring can only produce fragmented, superficial, and usually very costly changes. Changes in the way an organization thinks and how it activates and channels the energies of its people are not the result of shifting structure but of shifting the nature of working process.

The Behavioral Paradigm

Control over labor leads to external motivation

The machine paradigm enabled the rapid development of the industrial era, but at some point the speed and predictability of industrial machines outstripped the predictability of the people operating them. At this point, attention shifted from how to control the manufacturing process to how to control labor.

In the early twentieth century, psychologist John Watson persuaded leaders of industry to fund his research laboratory at Johns Hopkins University. He promised that his research would show them how to control people's behavior with the same level of scientific predictability and rigor that engineers were able to bring to the design of machinery. This work, which founded the discipline of behaviorism, was predicated on the belief that internal, subjective experience was irrelevant. The only phenomena that mattered were behaviors that could be objectively observed, categorized, and conditioned. Watson's research into *operant conditioning*, which was extended and elaborated by such well-known behaviorists as B. F. Skinner, had enormous impact later in the century on the field of work design, education, parenting, and advertising.[5]

Behavioral psychology is effective, in large part, because it taps into characteristics that humans share with many other animals. Through research on rats, primates, and other mammals, behaviorists were able to accurately describe how to condition people's behavior.

Like the aristocratic and mechanistic paradigms that preceded it, this approach assumes an outside authority whose goals drive all activity and thus shape employee behavior. It ignores and therefore fails to take advantage of many of the higher functions of human intelligence. Companies and all of their people have the innate potential for reflection and self-management, qualities they need to develop in order to move into the uncharted territories where innovation occurs. Business practices like the following, which are based on the premises of behavioral psychology, inevitably have far more negative than positive effects.

Incentive is the promise of a future reward, designed to stimulate a single-minded pursuit. For example, companies might promise salespeople a bonus for exceeding certain targets. An incentive generates a very specific stimulating effect on the brain by highlighting a gap between what people have and what they could have. This creates the compelling desire to close the gap, and thus serve as a source of energy to drive the development of desired behaviors and outcomes.

Because incentives trigger a primitive, engrained response, they produce a number of unintended consequences. First, they strongly reinforce self-aggrandizement, so much so that people can dedicate highly creative energy toward the counterproductive purpose of gaming the system. Second, they focus people's attention on the incentive, rather than on customers. Third, they reduce the sense of agency and locus of control in workers, placing it instead in the hands of those who are creating the incentives and providing the rewards. This not only undermines the ability to be self-managing, it also infantilizes people. Thus it is small wonder, given the ubiquity of this practice, that Americans struggle to see themselves as engaged, empowered participants in their own democratic institutions.

Rewards are designed to build and reinforce bonds of loyalty between workers and the superiors who bestow them. They can be distributed through incentive programs, but they can also arrive unexpectedly as the result of beneficence from above. In contrast to incentives, their effect on the brain is to reduce stimulation and satisfy desire, thereby producing a bond with the organization or person who doles them out.

Rewards subtly erode human character and relationships by valorizing dependency and self-serving loyalty over authenticity and the self-respect fostered within a community of equals. Organizationally, they contaminate a business culture by politicizing relationships, dividing people into competing camps of mutual benefit. In addition, they set in motion a downward spiral of dependency. As employees are less and less able to look to themselves to anticipate the needs of customers, each year they require management to provide them with increasingly explicit goals, incentives, and rewards to accomplish this basic work.

The irony is that the practice of giving rewards, which is so universally accepted as a way to improve performance, simply doesn't work. As Daniel Pink points out in his book *Drive*, research has shown time and again that rewards are only effective when it comes to the simplest and most menial tasks.[6] Anything that is complex and requires sustained effort depends on the development of people's intrinsic drive, which operates independently of external rewards. Yet, the belief that rewards are necessary to sustain motivation is so deep and unquestioned that people continue the practice throughout their social and professional institutions. They fail to understand how profoundly destructive it is to the development of free, independent, thoughtful, and democratic human beings, and they simply can't imagine an alternative.

Recognition is a special case of reward, wherein an authority figure singles out an individual or team and holds them up as exemplary with regard to how they work or what they have accomplished. Recognition programs reinforce a specific business culture by honoring those qualities that will earn workers love, acceptance, admiration, and emulation. As a rule, a business will use the recognition process as an opportunity to call out and instruct others in the qualities they are to cultivate in themselves if they are to be accepted members of the community.

Distinguishing particular people for recognition carries with it some very real hazards. First of all, no one is perfect, and shining a light on their accomplishments also opens them up to scrutiny by their peers with regard to their weaknesses, ultimately undermining the purpose of the reward. Second, no one does anything alone. When recognizing an individual or team, a business implicitly disregards the work of everyone else in the organization who contributed to their success, thereby leading to discontent, jealousy, and competitiveness.

Third, recognition encourages generic behaviors, thereby diminishing the richness and diversity of an organization's culture. By emphasizing one set of qualities as desirable, a company implicitly instructs its individual employees to abandon or sublimate the singular qualities that make them unique, setting them outside of group norms. But these qualities are the sources of passion and drive in individuals and the pathways by which innovation enters an organization. Singling out one individual or group for recognition has the effect of turning down the lights on all the others, depreciating the greater part of a company's most valuable assets.

Role modeling is based on identifying a living exemplar whose way of being should be emulated. Companies who adopt it as a primary management practice consider it to be critical for the development of leadership. A leader engages in exemplary behavior—often based on the life of an important historical figure, such as General George Patton or Eleanor Roosevelt—that others are expected to copy.

Role modeling has the same genericizing effect that recognition programs have. In addition, it feeds an unhealthy form of grandiosity in everyone who is asked to take it on. It sets them up to imagine that they are superior to others, a behavioral manifestation of the old aristocratic paradigm.

Rating and ranking is the foundation on which rewards, recognition, and role modeling are all based. Rating and ranking is carried out against the background of a set of standards and expectations established by the organization to govern the performance and behavior of its labor force.

Workers can be individually rated and then ranked in comparison to others with regard to their relative success in meeting these standards and expectations.

In a sense, rating and ranking provides the stick that goes with the carrots of reward and recognition. By incentivizing conformity to organizational norms and ideals, rating and ranking reinforces the corrosive loss of differentiation and individual creativity in a work force. Instead of seeing their business as an instrument for contributing to a better world, workers come to see themselves as instruments of an authoritarian will that requires them to give up their own unique identities and passions. In this way, the aristocratic and mechanistic paradigms reassert themselves through newer, more sophisticated psychological means.

Not surprisingly, innovation as a collective activity is impossible in a system that promotes conformity. This forces companies to establish specialized innovation programs staffed by innovation experts who do the work on behalf of the rest of the company. But in fact, this reduces the potential scope for innovation because no team of specialists can match the comprehensive view and collective intelligence of an entire organization. It also tends to limit innovation to product offerings, rarely addressing innovation in such things as operations, distribution, or customer service.

Performance reviews extend the mechanistic idea of feedback and standards into the behaviorist paradigm. As with feedback, a performance review starts from the assumption that the only way for workers to get an accurate view of their performance is to have other people tell them how they are doing. As with standards, a performance review assumes an external and objectively verifiable level of expected performance. Performance reviews, backed up by incentives and punishment, are designed to steer workers closer and closer to standardized ideals of behavior and results. Originally, the practice was an exclusively top-down activity, in which a superior reviewed the work of a subordinate, but it has shifted over time. Now it is often a participatory engagement in which subordinates incorporate their own perspective into the review. And an even more inclusive ordeal, known as 360-degree feedback, includes input from a worker's colleagues.

The minute a business standardizes assessment to an imposed review process, it obliterate the sense of agency and individuation in workers. Their work is carried out as mechanical activity inside a box, rather than as a creative and living response to emerging conditions. This box is usually formed by goals that are set at the beginning of the year, and these goals provide immediate limits within which work takes place, regardless of what is happening in the larger world. This places counterproductive limitations on the thinking of workers, who wish to receive good reviews and therefore focus on achieving the goals rather than take the risk of examining them and of seeming to question authority.

In addition, performance reviews trigger all of the same negative consequences as feedback, providing an enormous distraction for workers. Rather than looking outward to the larger effect that a company is trying to produce in the world and for its customers, workers look inward to their review. They waste time and spend psychological energy worrying about or arguing with its contents. Add to this the research demonstrating that reviews are inevitably skewed by unconscious personal and institutional bias, and the entire process can be seen to diminish energy, goodwill, and the likelihood that creative outliers will find ways to make useful contributions.[7,8,9] Happily, this view is becoming more generally accepted, and human resource divisions have begun to move away from the practice of employee reviews.

Market research and *customer feedback* are two practices that arose as local businesses grew into companies so large that they could no longer maintain direct contact with customers. Market research allowed companies to identify the needs and desires of customers and thus to steer the course of product development and improvement. The practice has evolved in sophistication, taking into account ethnographic information, demographic trends, and, of course, direct feedback from customers.

Yet inevitably, market research is only the application of the behavioral paradigm to customers. It assumes that consumers are like rats moving through a maze, motivated by rewards and looking for ways to get them more easily and consistently. And customers, unlike rats, can say where they are encountering difficulties running the maze. Based on their reports, the company can then shift its behavior and hope in return that customers will shift theirs.

As Steve Jobs has pointed out, consumers will tell you what annoys them or what they want right now, but they are almost never able to articulate what they aspire to achieve and what might help them get there.[10] This is why, as the Harvard Market Research Center has demonstrated, 80 percent of the information derived from surveys will fail to translate into sales.[11] The dirty secret about market research is that it makes people in a company lazy. Instead of generating deep thinking about directions customers are seeking to go in their lives, workers come to depend upon relatively useless information about where customers are right now. This becomes the basis for making bad and very expensive decisions about where to invest product development resources—decisions whose failures are blamed on almost everything but the original market research.

Universal training is useful and necessary for building skills. For example, when a company adopts a new software program to manage its internal systems, then it is necessary to train everyone to use it. However, training is not appropriate when it comes to the development of human creativity, motivation, or agency. These need to be awakened, not inculcated. They require a structured educational process, one that is experiential, developed through time, reflective, and based on independent discovery within the context of work application. Whereas training is a mechanical process that everyone goes through in more or less the same way, education is an individuating process that supports the development of unique capabilities. The role of an innovative organization is to create the conditions within which true education can take place.

The Human Potential Paradigm

Self-actualization leads to internal motivation

The aristocracy, machine, and behavioral paradigms emphasized the use of external controls (over ownership, process, or labor) as a means to move toward some ideal of performance. By the middle of the twentieth century, this emphasis on control was becoming increasingly out of step with a culture that was exploring the importance of human self-determination and self-expression. By the 1960s, this ferment had caused the rise of the human potential movement, led by such influential humanistic psychologists as Virginia Satir, Abraham Maslow, and Carl Rogers. They rejected a system that treated people as if they were merely tools, celebrating instead the idea that human beings were inherently worthy. In place of controls, they proposed self-direction; in place of optimization, they proposed actualization; and in place of the idea of humans as the tools of others, they proposed the pursuit of the potential inherent in each person.

The human potential movement effectively shifted a host of organizational systems toward a new view of the role of humans in work. These became far better able to tap the creativity and energy of employees, even as employees found their work to be more meaningful and satisfying. Still, by limiting its focus to the self-actualization of individuals, the human potential movement contained a fundamental blind spot. It kept the focus inward and human, which meant that it was unable to adequately take into account the relationship between humans and the larger systems that we interact with—especially the natural systems.

Perhaps the greatest issue that resulted from the adaptation of humanistic psychology to business had to do with the consultants who attempted to do the adapting. Steeped as they were in the mechanistic and behaviorist paradigms, they misunderstood the fundamental insight of the human potential movement—that humans needed to be the authors of their own choices and actions. Instead, they took the concept of human development to be simply a replacement for the concept of performance. As a result, the programs that they developed to apply the philosophy of humanism were profoundly colored by the techniques of behaviorism. Some of the most common programs based on humanist principles are described here, along with the main reasons why they don't work.

Surveys of organizational climate and culture are designed to help businesses develop an objective and unbiased understanding of how people feel about their overall work experience. The opinions of workers are solicited on everything from fairness in hiring and pay to the degree of personal fulfillment they receive from their work. The aim of all this is to engage the intelligence and self-determination of employees in order to help companies provide supportive work environments that improve their people's performance and motivation.

But like all such feedback processes, climate and culture surveys gather information about likes and dislikes within the frame of people's existing body of experience. As a rule, they invite superficial reactions rather than deep, creative thinking. This makes them anti-innovative because they add nothing to the kind of insight that would put an organization out in front of its workers' experience.

Even more important, surveys have the effect of separating workers from their own agency. Rather than encouraging co-responsibility for creating the conditions for meaningful work, surveys imply that someone else will take responsibility for the information that has been gathered. This usually leads to resentment, because by the time a complaint or suggestion makes its way through the organization and back to the employee, in the form of some new program, it bears little relationship to what was originally articulated. "Why do they ask me, if they don't intend to do anything about it," disgruntled employees think to themselves (and sometimes complain aloud).

Typologies of personality are used by companies as a way to manage the complexity that shows up whenever we begin to think of people as autonomous, self-managing individuals, rather than machine parts or lab rats. They sort and classify people, but not by background, training, or education. Instead they classify them according to personality or psychological traits, such as introverted and extroverted or analytical and synthesizing. In this way, the reasoning goes, programs and practices can be more closely tailored to their needs. Typologies are also intended to help people better understand themselves and one another in order to promote more harmonious working relationships.

Unfortunately, typologies simplify the unlimited diversity and changeability of human expression, and simplification is almost always a bad way to try to manage complexity. Also, they cannot be verified.

There is no scientific basis for the assertion that there are "four types of human mind" or "nine types" or "twelve types." This in itself wouldn't be an issue, if it weren't for the fact that typologies are fundamentally destructive in practice.

The real issue is that typologies are a method of generalization. The minute a business groups people into categories, it diminishes their unique individuality, which is the most sustainable source of their motivation and desire to contribute. It also puts a box around the workers' potential. Typologies emphasize the broad features that people have in common, while obliterating the subtler distinctions that differentiate them from one another. They perversely reinforce those broad commonalities at the expense of distinguishing differences, as people come to identify themselves with the category into which they have been placed. They also delimit the range of possible expressions, creating an artificial ceiling on what someone might aspire to become. For example, a person might conclude, "I'm a naturally messy thinker, so I could never be good at anything that requires attention to detail."

Participatory ideation seeks to promote an atmosphere of inclusiveness by soliciting the opinions and thoughts of employees, using methods like group process, suggestion boxes, or memos circulated to invite responses. Ideally, these methods give employees a sense that they are playing a role in the decision-making process, while greatly enriching the raw material that management draws on to make its decisions.

Participatory ideation falls apart precisely when it parts company from decision making, action, and evaluation. Employees are asked to contribute thoughts without any expectation or opportunity to follow through with actions, and this diminishes both their agency and their sense of responsibility for the quality of thinking generated. The problem is that *participation* is simply too passive, too low-level an activity for a company to ask of its employees. What's needed is a way of engaging, in which ideation, execution, and evaluation are undertaken as a single, seamless process. The quality and feasibility of ideas goes up and their tendency to create fragmentation goes down when people know that they will have to deliver on them.

Instant potential derives from the philosophy that everyone has the inherent capacity to rise to almost any occasion, if given the opportunity to sink or swim. Managers who operate from this philosophy give their employees major challenges and lots of leeway to figure them out. From this point of view, failure is an acceptable part of the process, since the whole point of the exercise is to get people to discover their potential through making the effort.

The problem here is the strong element of magical thinking in the idea that potential will manifest, full-blown and fully realized, in response to some challenge, as though it were controlled by an on-off switch. Actually, potential is open-ended. It grows over time as it is developed. A newborn infant is almost pure potential, but the realization of that potential requires parenting, socialization, education, and self-examination if it is to manifest.

In fact, there are several hazards associated with the idea of instant potential. The first is that throwing people into the deep end can quite literally traumatize them. It can actually destroy their potential. The second is that if businesses adopt the belief that potential can be activated by an on-off switch, then these institutions are relieved of their critical responsibility for providing the developmental culture within which potential actually flourishes. Businesses, if they truly want to unleash human potential, have to commit themselves to developing it, not just utilizing it.

Visioning taps the unique power of the frontal lobe of the human brain, which is able to project thoughts into the future. A visioning process invites people to generate a collective image of a better state that they want to move toward. Once this collective vision has come to life in people's minds, they will move mountains to try to bring it into reality. Small wonder that visioning processes have been so widely adopted by groups of every stripe as a way to chart a future direction.

However, in spite of their power, visioning processes in the workplace are deeply toxic. First of all, visions occur in the minds of individuals, not in groups. In order to translate those individual visions into a collective statement, the diversity of interpretations needs to be ironed out, with all of the areas of disagreement set aside. The result is a compromised pastiche cobbled together around what people are able to agree on.

Also, by inviting people to contemplate a better world, visioning processes implicitly start from what currently exists and ask people to improve upon it. Even "blue sky" processes, intended to promote openness to the wildest of possibilities, assume people's experience of what exists as the basis for their leaps of imagination.

At the same time, visioning processes fail to actually address reality. Because they are framed around questions about what kind of future people would like to see, they indulge people's human tendency to unconsciously project themselves onto the world. Visioning, in other words, subtly promotes the subjugation of nature and people by making the *desires* of the visioners the principle around which they organize.

Instead, people in businesses and other organizations should engage together in the process of *imaging the working of the living entities they wish to know and serve*, seeing them as mutually interactive aspects of a whole system. This has the advantage of decreasing ego involvement and preventing projections, and it is something groups can learn to do together early in a work design or other change process. Also, imaging can be extended to any effort to engage with an entity or entities within a living system. It will always improve outcomes.

Institutional ideals offer an aspirational measure of behavior or accomplishment that can be shared across an organization. They describe a pattern for people to emulate, a way of being that informs an organization's distinctive culture and world view. Ideals are intended to energize a workforce, providing a template toward which people can move: "We're energetic self-starters!" or "We get it right—first time, every time." They establish the boundary conditions that indicate who will fit well within a given organizational culture.

The long and celebrated history of human ideals, reaching back far beyond ancient Greece, carries buried within it the equally long history of their destructive potential. Ideals, after all, are inherently compulsory. People who can't meet the ideal are by definition failures, somehow less than. This is as true of our ideals of human beauty, skin color, speech patterns, and manners as it is of our ideals of business behavior. Ideals objectify—they impose norms and open the space within which one group despises, excludes, or shuns another.

By extension, this exclusionary space limits the potential for individuated growth and development and therefore genuinely individual invention. As long as workers are striving to achieve someone else's ideal, they are diverted from pursuing the expression of their own individual potential. This cuts them off from the source of their creativity and, therefore, from the contribution that they alone could make to the future of their organization. As with so many other practices that seek to create a common standard, institutional ideals undermine human innovation.

As a side note, it's important to point out that principles and ideals are not the same thing, although they are both intended to cultivate aspiration. Ideals are fixed, and thus they act in opposition to differentiation and evolution. Principles, on the other hand, are open-ended and encourage ongoing exploration and human development.

Here's an example of the difference. When I first worked with DuPont, the company held a strong ideal of safety, expressed as zero tolerance for accidents. Not surprisingly this produced an atmosphere of anxiety, especially given the company's history of firing any manager who experienced a serious accident on his or her watch. Perversely, this was leading to an increase in accidents.

We proposed a principle to replace this ideal: "An increasingly safe workplace every day." Instead of starting the day by asking workers, "How safe were we overnight?" plant managers began to ask them to report on a different question: "How did we improve safety yesterday?" This shift in emphasis turned safety into something that people could engage with creatively. Instead of a fixed ideal, safety became something that had no upper limit, an arena within which innovation could flourish.

Human-centered design grew out of the recognition that older paradigms had focused entirely on the efficient accomplishment of tasks, leaving the higher needs of human beings almost entirely out of the picture. The human potential movement set out to address this oversight by working on everything from comfort and ergonomics in the workplace to problem-solving participation as a way for employees to derive meaning and satisfaction from their work. Taken together, these strategies create a far more hospitable work environment for human beings.

As good as it may be, though, human-centered design leaves out one of the most critical prerequisites to a genuinely innovative work culture: a focus on stakeholders. Like most of the innovations of the human potential movement in general, human-centered design is focused inward: "As long as we keep our people happy, everything else will fall into place." But this inward focus necessarily limits the amount of meaning that work can provide.

Until people develop their capacity to focus their attention on the evolution of those larger stakeholder systems that lie outside of themselves, the deep or disruptive innovation that makes work truly meaningful lies outside their grasp. Although the insights of the human potential movement have been extremely important for growing more humane working environments, they are no longer sufficient to meet the need for profound changes in the world today.

Detoxifying Your Business

I meet people on a regular basis who express enthusiastic interest in adding new tools to their toolbox. They can see the power of the practices I recommend and want to learn how to integrate them into the work they are doing. "Sorry," I have to tell them. "I'm afraid I can't help you with that."

A regenerative approach is systemic and based on a coherent worldview or paradigm. It can't be bolted onto an existing work design that was built out of toxic practices and derived from antiquated paradigms. Why would you want to drag the old destructive patterns into the different future that you are trying to create? You might be able to achieve a few improvements here and there, but the transformational benefits of a regenerative work design would be lost.

In order to work in a regenerative way, you need to clear the decks of old, toxic practices and the mindsets from which they arose. For example,

I know of many companies that have encountered the concept of promises beyond ableness in one of my books or lectures and loved the idea. But when they try to implement it for themselves, they almost always create a program designed like all their other programs. They give employees instruction on how to select tasks, they provide incentives for those who successfully complete them, and they train people in the core competencies that they will need. In other words, by hanging on to old paradigms, they take a concept that has the potential to completely transform their business and use it to reinforce pre-existing blinders.

Real promises beyond ableness have their origins within the workers themselves. The driver is intrinsic—the caring and creativity that can be found in any human being—rather than external in the form of some top-down program through which people are marched. A company that wants to foster promises beyond ableness needs to create the conditions for workers to have their *own* discoveries about what customers really need and to experience the awakening of their *own* will to do something about it. But creating the conditions for personal agency and authority requires dismantling the machineries of compulsion, feedback, and hierarchical authority. Once workers have discovered their own guiding star, they will organize themselves to grow the capabilities they need to be able to follow it.

In part 2 I have laid out the criteria and conditions for a regenerative business, along with many of the most toxic practices that you will need to weed out in order to make your business regenerative. In part 3 I will lead you through the change process required for building a regenerative business.

CHAPTER SIX

Design a Developmental Organization

The conventional definition of management is getting work done through people, but real management is developing people through work.

Agha Hasan Abedi, Banker and Philanthropist

THERE'S A MYTH OUT THERE that people naturally hate and fear change. It's simply not true. Human beings are designed for change. It's built into the frontal lobes of our brains, which allow us to project future possibilities that we can barely resist pursuing. What people hate is the sense that change is inflicted on them—that they are victims of circumstance and have no ability to participate in shaping the future that they are being dragged into.

Unfortunately, most business leaders, educators, and consultants have an overly simplistic view of what change is, how it occurs, and how people should be engaged with it. Most change efforts are imposed from the outside. From this perspective, change is a process of rearranging external circumstances: change people's titles, where they sit, the lighting they work in, who they report to, and the incentives to which they are subjected. Even when the reasons for the change effort are excellent, an external approach triggers a natural and completely appropriate resistance from those on whom it is imposed.

Real change arises from the desire and agency of individuals who see an audacious possibility on their horizon and are willing to try almost anything to make it happen. This is the natural state of human beings when they are given opportunities to be self-determining and to access and develop the full creative potential of their own minds. For this reason, a developmental change process creates *conditions* in the form of bold, disruptive initiatives, while supporting the development of the *capabilities* people will need to successfully pursue them.

As developmental business leaders, our task is to build adventurous business cultures. We aim to awaken in people the sheer fun and excitement of walking a tightrope together, of trying things that have never been done before in order to create results that are almost unimaginably powerful. This is what our work designs need to deliver: companies for whom change is simply a way of life.

Developing Whole Human Beings

In my practice of work design, I always bear in mind that humans are multidimensional. I have found three critical learning principles that are necessary guides for the kind of human development program that regenerative work systems are based on.

First, *human development comes through education rather than instruction*. That is, it needs to be designed to draw people out rather than cram things into their brains—to build their critical-thinking skills rather then spoon feed them content. Real education focuses on individual learning and discovery, rather than packaged content. It does this by introducing premises and frameworks that challenge people's habitual thinking patterns. It then insists that they test these foundational ideas in terms of their own experience to ascertain for themselves the concepts' validity. Out of this, people become increasingly able to generate new patterns of thinking that can be applied to their work. This kind of teaching cannot be preprogrammed—there are no best teaching practices—and thus to do it well is a tall order for the educator. However, if we want to grow people who are able to walk tightropes, creatively responding to what's happening in the present moment, then our education processes also need to mirror what it looks like to walk a tightrope.

Second, when people come to an educational session, they need to be *working on real business endeavors with their natural working team so that together they can implement what they've learned and planned immediately upon leaving the room.* This contrasts with what I call "cold storage" training programs, which teach skills that will be used some time in the future. For example, communications skills are often taught through packaged programs, in which everyone gets the same training. These skills may be important, but because they aren't tied to specific activities for specific people at specific moments in time, they lack immediacy and relevance. Working from reality cultivates in people the ability to make real decisions in real time.

Third, *the development of people is directly tied to their ability to make a difference in the lives of customers,* those individuals and communities that a business exists to serve. This is the true, sustaining source of motivation and will for workers. It gives them the experience that their work is worthwhile. Helping workers connect their thinking to what's good for customers is the whole purpose of the educational sessions. By applying critical thinking to the question of how to improve the lives of specific people, workers generate their own learning content, insights, and decisions about what actions to take. This gives them a way to channel their creative energies and personal growth into work that will benefit everyone.

Phases in Work Design

Whether for individuals or institutions, transformational change takes strong effort. The almost overwhelming tendency to slip back into habitual ruts and well-worn ways of working competes in people's minds with the initial motivation to change. Thus, all those who are evolving regenerative organizations need to accept that profound change requires growth through time as they pass through subsequent phases of development. This is why training programs are inadequate to the task. It takes more than a new skill or insight to transform behavior; it takes a developmental process supported by the right organizational conditions.

Many change programs are based on the mistaken assumption that change is material: a simple move from point A to point B. As a result, they tend to be focused on restructuring—reworking the chain of command, reorganizing departments, remodeling the workplace. But this is the most expensive and least effective way to work on change.

In chapters 7 through 11, I offer a completely different way of thinking about designing for change. I suggest a series of five phases that starts by drawing people in and building their capabilities. This lets them seize ownership of the change process from the beginning, and it guarantees that they have confidence in their ability to carry it out. Instead of resisting and fearing change as some kind of personal threat, they become advocates for transformations that will make a difference in the world and produce a stronger business.

It might be worth spending a moment examining what I mean by *phase*. Phases are generally thought of as unfolding sequentially through time. While this is true, it is more accurate to think of them as nested inside one another, so that even as people work on one phase, they are setting the stage for work on all the following. For example, a young musician starts out learning scales and exercises that develop basic technical proficiency. As it begins to bear fruit, this phase doesn't end. Instead, the focus shifts and the next phase—learning to play increasingly difficult pieces of music—moves into the foreground. This phase is followed by the next and the next. The musician learns to subordinate technical skill to the underlying requirements of phrasing and expressivity, to harmonize with other musicians, and so on. Meanwhile, in the background the work on scales and exercises continues, becoming ever more productive through time.

There Are No Recipes

In the introduction to this book, I emphasized that redesigning work is about "intentionally generating something new, something that responds creatively to the specific needs and opportunities of a business, its customers, and its employees." I explained my desire to avoid introducing yet another off-the-shelf program with standard procedures and a recipe for producing results. By now it should be apparent to readers that doing so would be antithetical to the development of a regenerative business.

My intention all along has been to help you create an image for yourself of what is possible, anchored by criteria and conditions that allow it to be conceptually whole and coherent. My aim, after all, is to help you set out on your own, wildly creative path.

It is in this spirit that I offer the following chapters. The phases I describe and the ways I think about them are derived from my own experience. The thread that runs through them and allows them to be holographic is the development of whole human beings. If you decide to take these phases on, you will be able to elaborate upon and extend my thinking from your own experience—but only so long as you pay attention to the developmental processes that you and your organization are undertaking. To support you in this creative learning, each chapter closes with a structured series of guiding questions.

CHAPTER SEVEN

Phase One—Evolve into Strategic Disruption

By doing what they must do to keep their margins strong and their stock price healthy, every company paves the way for its own disruption.

Clayton M. Christensen, Author of *How Will You Measure Your Life?*

THE PURPOSE OF THE FIRST PHASE of regenerative work design is to destabilize an organization by introducing a provocation that causes people to think from radically new perspectives. I call this a *conscious shock* for two reasons. It's *conscious* because it invites people to remember the origins and purpose of their work and to discover meaningful new ways to express these in the world. It's a *shock* because it also makes people aware of how conditioned the organization has become, how mechanically reactive it is to outside forces, and how easily it loses connection to its authenticity. A conscious shock often takes the form of a question intended to wake people up from their unconscious habits of thought so they can become more conscious of what is true about themselves and their world.

Five Phases of Innovative Work Disruption

A successfully applied conscious shock challenges familiar routines and shakes people out of their comfort zones. Yet it does this without introducing any sense of threat to their identity or position. Rather, it connects them to the essence of who they are, as individuals and as a company, and to the essence of their customers. It takes them into the big world that lies beyond their job descriptions. In other words, it helps them learn to adopt the perspective of a CEO.

The Core Team

It takes time to introduce a conscious shock across an entire organization. In practical terms, a business leader makes this possible by setting up a *core team*, whose purpose is to grow the business. The first step of the core team's work is to dismantle the tradition of hierarchical decision making. Of course, this requires a great deal of courage from the leader, who must be willing to redefine leadership and decision making completely apart from the conventional notions of bosses and workers. A colleague of mine used to say that the only business leaders who can do this are those who no longer need ego satisfaction from their work and are willing to dedicate themselves to making a difference in the lives of their stakeholders. For a lot of executives, this would be a deal breaker. But for some, it's the most uplifting challenge of their careers.

The core team's role is to keep the organization and its people awake. Core team membership cuts across all hierarchical boundaries—departments, levels, perspectives, and experience—in order to reflect the whole of the business. Unlike traditional cross-functional, multilevel teams—which are intended to enable a participative process for carrying out defined tasks—a core team is chartered to develop and execute significantly new business strategies that will make the company nondisplaceable in its market. Of course, a radically new strategy requires a radically new planning process, and a critical part of the core team's work has to do with learning and applying innovative approaches to strategy development.

The core team is chartered to learn how to think systemically and strategically and to channel this new knowledge directly into transformational change. Members are selected for their interest in developing themselves, their willingness to engage others in learning, and their respected leadership abilities. They are not representatives; they are not elected, and they are not expected to represent the opinions of a particular group. Rather, they are expected to use their diverse perspectives to generate understanding about how each aspect of the business influences and participates in the strategic direction of the whole.

In my experience, the work with core teams is deeply shocking (in a good way) for its members. They start out with that deer in the headlights look, hardly able to believe what I'm asking them to do. But within a few short months they are ready and eager to take on far more complex challenges than the ones we started with and have developed the habit of thinking about the whole of the business. This excitement is contagious and quickly begins to be communicated across the company.

The Core Team's First Task

The first and most important task of the core team is to help the entire company shift the way it thinks about who it is in relationship to its customers. This requires upending conventional practices of market research, which deliver *knowledge* about customers but very little *understanding* of what it's like to live their lives. Market data can shed light on various aspects of customer behaviors or preferences, but it doesn't help businesses see the customers as a whole.

The core team learns how to pursue a direct and unmediated experience of what's going on in the customers' lives. What are they aspiring to do? What challenges do they face? What kind of help could the business provide that would actually make a difference for the customers? The concrete sense of what it's like to stand in the customers' shoes awakens a strong sense of caring among core team members. It gives them a powerful inner compass with regard to the kind of actions that customers would perceive to be truly useful or meaningful. This same caring for the customers can be awakened in others, and it is one of the core team's primary responsibilities to invite their coworkers to join them in becoming curious about their customers' lives.

The core team also learns to understand the business itself as a unique, living, and purposeful system. Questions they ask themselves include the following:

- Where did we come from, and where should we be going?
- What is the essence of our organization, the thing that enables us to make our own distinctive contribution to our market?
- What are our values with regard to helping create a healthy society and planet? Based on our answers, how will our organization set a common direction that allows us to become a singular, unified, and powerful force in the world?

When a company is able to put its unique character to work in order to anticipate what will truly serve its customers, it becomes nondisplaceable to them. It becomes a trusted source and ally, and as long as it keeps faith with the customers, they will remain loyal. This kind of thinking is the basis for strategies that can transform not only a company, but everything it touches.

The core team carries out its work through an open process, so that as members develop new insights and new ways of working, they are continuously sharing these with their departments and fellow workers. In this way, the company as a whole is learning alongside the core team and contributing to the development of strategic thinking.

In company after company that I have worked with, the effect of awakening creative intelligence in the workforce is like an earthquake. Workers stop thinking of themselves in static terms: "I'm a doer who knows how to do my job well." Instead, they begin to see themselves dynamically: "I'm a developer and an innovator. I challenge myself to go beyond my past achievements, so that I can help evolve what's possible in the future."

This shift in orientation from static to dynamic produces a risk-taking culture and develops workers with the agency to be self-directing rather than dependent on direction from above. It is radical in its effect and implications. Employees need time and practice to do it well, but once they develop strategic thinking capabilities, they become able to respond creatively to whatever is happening inside and outside the organization, even as the market and the world changes around them.

Merida Meridian

Merida Meridian is a Boston-based textile design and manufacturing company that has successfully tapped the creativity of its workforce to create products that are both luxurious and sustainable. In the course of four years, it transformed itself from a conscientious and mission-driven—but basically invisible—company to an award-winning industry leader. The story behind that transformation started with a conscious shock.

Catherine Connolly, Merida Meridian's founder and owner, originally approached me because she'd heard that I help companies do great storytelling. She thought this would be a useful capability to develop for her marketing. I met with several members of her leadership team and immediately asked them a basic question: "Who are you and what makes you unique?"

They answered, "Sustainability!"

I explained, "That hardly makes you unique; most businesses are trying to be sustainable these days."

Slowly it dawned on them that they were defining themselves in terms of their mission, not their essence. At a deep level, they didn't actually know who they were, and therefore they couldn't tell an authentic story about themselves. This was their first conscious shock.

My second big question was, "What are your customers' strategies for differentiating themselves, and what makes you important to them?"

Again, their answers were generic and, therefore, imprecise. They were dismayed to discover that they didn't know their customers well enough to discern their essences. Instead of understanding their customers by how they lived their lives and did their work, Merida Meridian's leaders did what most business leaders do: they sorted customers by demographics and size of account. This made it nearly impossible to care about them.

When the leadership team realized this and began to see their customers as real people whom they could care deeply about, they received a second conscious shock, and suddenly they were ready to go to work. That was when we agreed to set up a core team to spread this inquiry across the organization.

As the team began to develop strategic thinking together, they realized that Merida Meridian's current business model was in conflict with both its essence and with its natural customers. The company had been supplying retailers who used it as a contract producer, hiding its brand and its creativity. But Merida Meridian's work force was made up of master weavers and dyers, many of whom were refugees and immigrants to the United States who had been greatly celebrated in their native lands. These craftspeople were capable of producing exceptionally high-value products, when given the opportunity. This realization pointed the core team toward Merida Meridian's essence: *a company of artisans who were innovating with regard to their craft.*

At the same time, the company's customers were also creative people: designers whose ability to express themselves was hampered by the relatively generic offerings of national retailers. Through a process of imaging customers in their work, the core team was able to differentiate among these designers. They identified four key groups: Bespoke (establishing their own brand with unique, one-of-a-kind products); Eclectic (drawing from different cultures and eras to tell a compelling story); Trendsetters (on the cutting edge with regard to color, pattern, and style); and Classicists (focused on quality and historic authenticity). Suddenly, the idea of innovation became meaningful: "How can we surprise the designers in each of these classes? How can we give them something beyond what they have thought of asking for? How can we help them be successful in the niche that they want to occupy?"

Early in the process, the core team came up with a game-changing idea. They established design studios where artisans and customers could work together to come up with new patterns and new weaving and dying methods, even new ways of putting looms together. The Merida Meridian team visited their customers' showrooms to gather images, ideas, and inspiration for the kinds of innovations that would be needed in the coming season. Before long, customers were counting on Merida Meridian to be their partners in research, development, and design.

This strategy carried big risks because it meant ending their relationships with current distributors and launching into a completely new, unmediated way of working with designers. To do it, the organization had to build the capacity of everyone in the company to understand the businesses of the four designer classes and what they were trying to achieve. Not surprisingly, working with and for specific designers inspired the pride and the talents of Merida Meridian's unique workforce, and it enabled the company to triple its margins in less than two years.

Recommendations

I've said before that a regenerative business can't be built by procedures. There is no recipe for you to follow. Instead, you need to learn the general patterns involved and then discover through experience how to adapt them to your own company. The work of creating a regenerative business is governed by the following overarching purpose:

> *To create the organizational framework that will inextricably link our development and expression of human potential to the evolution of business effectiveness.*

Under this governing purpose, the five phases are distinct. Each must be designed to produce particular outcomes, using appropriate means and methods while growing the requisite capabilities. The following questions are intended to help you develop a design for phase one.

Questions to Address Outcomes

- What seemingly insurmountable restraints do our customers face that our company might creatively address as a way to establish a strong bond of loyalty?

- Who are we as a company? What is it about us that makes us the perfect organization to take on these opportunities?

- What corporate direction will demand boldness from every one of us in the pursuit of unique, innovative products and services that will elevate the capacity of our customers to pursue their dreams?

Questions to Address Means and Methods

- What clarity and inspiration will we build into our core team's charter to empower it to set the course for this new corporate direction while simultaneously growing the capability of all team members?

- Who needs to be on the core team to reflect the multiplicity of perspectives found across the organization?

- What managing principles are needed to guide this team in its achievements and growth?

Questions to Address Capabilities

- How will we learn to engage in and then act from external considering with regard to our customers? How will we make this an ongoing conversation in all teams across the company?

- What practices do we have in our organization that are likely to be toxic in this phase? How will we begin to move away from them?

- How will we help everyone in the organization discover the places where they can apply these insights in order to improve what they are working on now?

CHAPTER EIGHT

Phase Two—Evolve a Courageous Culture

Culture eats strategy for lunch.

Peter Drucker, Father of Modern Management

THROUGH ITS ONGOING PRACTICES, the culture of an organization holds in place the patterns of belief that dictate or proscribe behavior. Culture is the water we swim in, manifested and sustained in our activities and the ways we work, and thus it is so pervasive that it can easily become invisible to us. However, to make real change in an organization, it is necessary to change its culture. And if we want to create a new culture, we need to change the ways we work—in every activity, every day.

Five Phases of Innovative Work Disruption

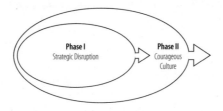

Often, companies try to work on culture change by making structural changes. For example, they might decide to get rid of supervisors or eliminate performance reviews or implement 360-degree feedback. The irony is that the way these decisions come down through the hierarchy tends to reinforce the existing culture. Also, because they are usually imported from outside the company and are almost always imposed from above, such efforts stimulate resistance, passive compliance, or both.

Deep culture creation, the kind that is needed to grow innovative organizations, happens through experience, education, and reflection, not through imposition. Once leaders have disrupted existing patterns in phase one, they are positioned to introduce new, more holistic ways of working. As employees experience the power and creativity that flow from a shift in approach, they become increasingly enthusiastic about extending this experience into other aspects of their work lives. This begins to dissolve the old culture and allows a new one to emerge in its place. It happens naturally, from the ground up, powered by the excitement and volition of workers.

For example, core team members take what they've learned back into their natural working teams. With their colleagues, they develop the capability to make decisions based on the overall character and direction of the company and the benefits that it is trying to bring into customers' lives. This encourages them to think in terms of wholeness, rather than in terms of fragments and provides an antidote to conventional analytical or reductionist approaches. Rather than start from problems, breaking them into their component parts in order to generate solutions, teams build their systemic thinking capabilities. The creative power they are able to harness becomes a strong incentive for them to do more. Such approaches, as they are brought more and more into daily activities, begin to shift people's experience of what life can be like in their organization. In other words, they begin to grow a new culture.

Characteristics of a Regenerative Culture

Six cultural characteristics will always be present in a regenerative company, though they will manifest differently depending on different company essences.

Imperturbability in the Face of Uncertainty

A regenerative business wholeheartedly embraces the reality of a changing market and world. Because it strives to innovate in ways that will anticipate and define these changes, it is inevitably venturing into the unknown. This needs to be a source of inspiration and excitement for employees, not a source of dread. Thus, everything about the business culture needs to develop the workers' ability to remain imperturbable and engaged, even as they encounter wicked curve balls.

Purposefulness Beyond Reproach

For me, purpose is not something that people have; it is something that people serve. In other words, it is the opposite of self-aggrandizement; it always comes from the benefits people deliver to something other than themselves. In a regenerative business context, these benefits need to ripple out, so that customers are better able to serve their own larger purposes (for example, the intention to be a good parent, citizen, or business person).

Purposefulness becomes beyond reproach when it shows up over and over again as the defining pattern of a business's operations. As a customer, I develop deep trust in certain businesses because I can see that they have consistently placed my well-being above all other priorities. Even when they make mistakes, I am prepared to give them the benefit of the doubt because I recognize the clear pattern of purposefulness in their actions.

Developmental Means

The word *development* comes from Latin: *to remove the veil.* When an organization dedicates itself to developmental means, it seeks to remove the external conditions and internal mental habits that prevent people from expressing who they are truly capable of becoming.

In a regenerative business culture, change leaders see their colleagues and employees as individuals with potential that can be developed, rather than as problems to be solved or managed. These leaders learn to see the new capabilities that people will need to grow if they are to fulfill their potential, and they devote their energies and talents to ensuring that opportunities are provided for this development to occur.

This takes root in a company once it recognizes that people's potential is only realized when they are working to make something actual. In other words, learning something new doesn't happen in isolation from their actual work. Their work is what they are learning to do in a different way, and they design their projects to be sure that new capabilities and capacity are among the outputs.

Unfortunately, many companies don't realize that burnout occurs when people don't have the opportunity to grow themselves. Hopelessness arises when their capabilities cannot find expression. A regenerative business heals this unnecessary separation.

Regenerative Thinking

Regenerative thinking is a rigorous discipline. It demands that people concentrate as they seek to understand what is at the core of how something works. This is the opposite of brainstorming, which is expansive, undisciplined, and almost never anchored to any specifics about how something actually operates in a given context.

Regenerative thinking also demands that workers be present and creative—generating new thoughts rather than recycling thoughts that they've had before. Unlearning nonregenerative habits of thought takes effort and patience, which is why it is so helpful to have a regenerative culture to support employees in their development.

Unifying Strategy

When people have a shared focus, they gain confidence in their ability to stay on the same path, even as they are pursuing diverse initiatives. This encourages self-direction in decision making and action taking. It also helps eliminate fragmentation of focus because it links every aspect of work back to a single origin.

Thus, to be unifying, a strategy must reflect the essence of a business. It needs to be authentic, arising from what the organization uniquely has to offer. It also needs to clarify what is worth taking on: the focused pursuits that will have a significant effect in the market and in the world. Finally, it needs to be ubiquitous. Instead of distributing tasks and information on a need-to-know basis, a regenerative business assumes that everyone in the organization needs to know the strategy and their role within it. This enables them to undertake work responsibilities in ways that will creatively advance the company.

Self-to-Self Relationships

In a regenerative business, it is critical to foster the ability of everyone to think together, regardless of background, experience, or education. Thinking together, which grows organizational intelligence, is extremely difficult to do in conventional hierarchies, which promote role-to-role relationships (manager to subordinate, investor to executive, representative to customer, and so on). The roles mask the underlying humanity and authenticity of people, imposing artificial constraints on their caring and creativity.

In a regenerative business, self-to-self relationships are supported by the use of systemic frameworks that enable diverse people to think together about complex questions. Using frameworks, colleagues from throughout an organization can build on each other's work, while challenging one another to become more comprehensive and innovative in their thinking.

These six characteristics of a regenerative culture are not givens. They must be grown and sustained. For this reason, they need to be embodied, consciously and unconsciously, through a company's rituals and taboos, its symbols, and its signifiers.

Seventh Generation

Jeffrey Hollender, founder and CEO of Seventh Generation, had already made up his mind that he wanted to work with me to grow the company's ability to impact how business is done generally, while at the same time building a better platform for its own success. But he also wanted to give his executive team an opportunity to make the decision for themselves.

"Not a good idea," I told him. "That will start you down the wrong path, because you'll make the decision to create a new culture in a way that reinforces the old one. If you want to do regenerative work, then you will need to bring together a group that reflects the whole of the organization to make the decision."

That's what he did. Hollender invited people from across the company to experience what it might be like to work regeneratively. He didn't know it at the time, but he was forming a proto-core team. Even before we had begun substantive work, we'd started manifesting the pattern of a regenerative culture.

In our very first session, I introduced the group to a systemic framework that was designed to disrupt patterns of thinking and relating. I told them explicitly that they were responsible for generating thoughts that they had never had before. It probably won't surprise you to hear that they found this disconcerting. After all, they expected me to make a sales pitch! I let them know that this wasn't about me; it was about what they were trying to do for their business.

"We begin working on the business now," I said. "From that you will get a feel for working with me. I'm not here to talk you into something." I was there to educate them about how to grow people as a basis from growing financial effectiveness and industry influence. At the same time, I was using our interaction to initiate work on culture change. We spent two days together working as a team, developing a host of new ideas for evolving their business. At the end, I asked them, "What was it like to come up with an answer that you weren't sure about and put it out there in front of the top management of your company? And for you managers, what was it like to expose your first ideas to your employees?"

Most of them replied, "Now that you mention it, we didn't even notice. It seemed completely natural. That's kind of remarkable!"

Then I asked, "And what was it like to use a framework to focus and bring discipline to your thinking?"

Hollender jumped in, obviously excited by what he was seeing. "It made us realize how much we think only about parts and pieces. We work on problems, which keep us locked into very small questions and prevent us from ever becoming strategic. Every time we tried to answer your questions about how our market works, you interrupted us. For example, when someone said that our customers make their decisions based on relative price, you pushed to get us to see that we weren't actually experiencing how our customers live. There is so much more here that we have to learn."

I continued to challenge their traditional process. "Okay, what's different about what we're doing here? What do you want to remember from this and integrate into the way you work?"

They pondered for a while, and then one group member ventured, "Well, first of all, we just shifted the power structure. Every one of us contributed to the thinking, and every one of us is capable of communicating it out. That implies a much higher level of shared responsibility than we've ever experienced before.

"Second, you didn't ask us for our ideas; you asked us to think systemically. That's going to have major implications for how we engage our coworkers and maybe even our customers.

"And finally, you invited us to look at ourselves so that we could notice our own thinking and how we could improve it. We've never encountered that before, at least not in business."

It wasn't hard to get these folks to agree to be on a core team because they'd already had the experience of what it was like. Over the following year, alongside our work on strategy, we examined the toxic practices that the organization had unwittingly engaged in since its founding. Although Seventh Generation had always conceived itself as a socially and environmentally conscious company, it was still burdened by received wisdom about how companies are supposed to work. Yet many of these conventional business practices were toxic to the company's culture. It was going to be important to stop doing some things and start doing new things to replace them.

The changes we made can be understood in terms of four critical cultural domains. As defined in anthropology, these are *status*, *symbol*, *ritual*, and *taboo*, and it turns out that they are as relevant to business as they are to any other culture. Here are the questions we examined:

- What does the organization give status to—what gets the most attention, the biggest budget, and the most recognition?

- What are the symbols that shape the business's sense of identity and role in the world?

- What has the company ritualized in ways that bind it to a particular path?

- What boundaries has the organization set around what is or is not acceptable, and what are the taboos by which these boundaries are kept in place?

For example, Seventh Generation used standardized performance reviews, a bit like report cards from school. This is how it was unconsciously assigning status to certain behaviors. Not only did this reinforce top-down decision making and undermine internal locus of control, it also treated all employees as if they were generic, working on the same things with the same expected results.

In its new culture, Seventh Generation was aiming to grow a community of self-determining, creative individuals with the understanding and confidence to take action on behalf of customers. So the core team eliminated performance reviews. Instead, employees received support to create their own self-defined and self-managed developmental work plan, along with a design for how they would audit, evaluate, and evolve the effects they were able to produce.

In another example, Seventh Generation had always held the belief that it was important for employees to feel that work was personally meaningful. It had acted on this belief by allowing all employees to dedicate some of their work time to gathering colleagues around an issue of mutual importance. This had become a kind of collective ritual. However, because the program lacked any connection to the overall strategic direction of the company, it scattered people's focus. In other words, the program encouraged personal agency, but it failed to develop internal locus of control and external considering.

The core team decided to address this problem in an unusually holistic way, by evolving a new companywide ritual of personal development. Once a month, everyone in the company participated in a daylong session focused on improving their thinking and capacity to self-manage. They would gather in their natural work teams, focusing on something that they were trying to accomplish together. This not only built personal capabilities, it greatly improved the teams' working dynamics. Collaboration went through the roof, as people learned to set their egos aside in order to pursue challenging goals.

Seventh Generation had always symbolized itself as David in a struggle with the Goliaths of the household products and personal care industry. The aim was figuratively to put themselves out of business by shifting the industry to the place where all companies were doing the right thing. But doing the right thing had been framed narrowly in terms of environmental impact. After only a few sessions, we began to redefine what was right in terms of *enhancing the lives of consumers*. Suddenly the company had a basis for truly transforming the industry, not through battle but through service. In other words, the symbols by which it conceptualized its identity had gone through a subtle but profound shift—from defeating the giant to serving him, from David and Goliath to Aesop's mouse and lion.

This reframing had another powerful influence on Seventh Generation's culture. Because the company had defined itself in relationship to the big players in its industry, it had also been unconsciously adopting their value systems. For example, Seventh Generation elevated the status of outside expertise in its decision making, especially with regard to market research. This led to an unconscious taboo against injecting personal, subjective experience into decisions.

Once I helped them see the deleterious effect this had on actually understanding and caring about their customers, the team quickly reversed the pattern. They replaced the old taboo with a new principle: *test the outside information we receive against our own experience*. They built online discussion boards that allowed them to have direct contact with consumers, and their ability to reflect from experience became increasingly accurate and nuanced.

Recommendations

Creating a culture, the work of phase two in the design of a regenerative work plan, has to do with the conscious evolution of your business culture so that it is increasingly well-aligned with the regenerative organization you are becoming. This means directly addressing the status, symbols, rituals, and taboos that you choose to adopt as a working community. You may have noticed in the Seventh Generation example that this work started to happen in our phase one. Right from the start, we began to dissolve the hold of the old culture in order to evolve something new in its place.

The following questions are intended to help you become more conscious and rigorous as you undertake this creative process.

Questions to Address Status

- What must we give status to, given our new focus and direction?
- What are we giving status to currently that will undermine our new direction?
- What is our plan to move from where we are now to where we want to be?

Questions to Address Symbols

- What metaphors or symbols fill our dialogues and drive our decision making (e.g., sports metaphors, biblical stories)?
- What is the impact on our culture of this form of storytelling?
- What are the new stories and metaphors that we choose to live by?

Questions to Address Rituals

- What routines do we engage in that appear to be meaningless to most people? Do any of these need to be preserved but imbued with new meaning?
- Which routines need to be eliminated? In eliminating them, is there some original intention that needs to be addressed in a new way?

- Where do we want to place new focus and meaning, and how do we create rituals to do that?

Questions to Address Taboos

- What actions or behaviors are most likely to get people shunned or expelled from our organization, even when the rules they break have never been explicitly stated? How do these taboos maintain the existing power structure and/or our attachment to a particular identity?

- What was the originating source of these taboos? Did they start out with a rational purpose (for example, fostering order and cohesion)? Alternatively, were they based on blind prejudice (for example, racism or sexism)?

- What are the managing principles that would address the need for order and cohesion while steering our intention to the new corporate direction?

CHAPTER NINE

Phase Three—Evolve People and Thinking Processes

You might think you're thinking your own thoughts. You're not. You're thinking your culture's thoughts.

Jiddu Krishnamurti, Philosopher

PROCESS REFERS TO HOW PEOPLE THINK, act, and interact. Processes occur in real time, within the changing circumstances of the real world. They are not procedures. One of the unfortunate residues of the mechanistic way of thinking is that most organizations try to turn *processes*, which are alive and based on what is happening in the moment, into *procedures*, which are predetermined. Processes require people to be present and awake. Procedures put people to sleep and make them mechanical. If you have ever been a customer trying to deal with a balky service representative at a large company, then you are probably familiar with how frustrating it can be to try to resolve your issue with someone who is only authorized to follow procedures.

Five Phases of Innovative Work Disruption

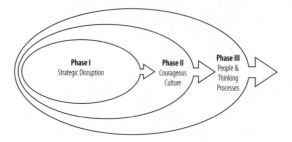

One of my mentors, Charles Krone, used to say, "If you don't see the world in process terms, you don't see the world." He meant that everything is particular and everything is changing all of the time. The raw materials used in a manufacturing process, the needs of particular customers, the impact of political or economic events on people's outlook and behaviors—these are all living phenomena, and they must be respected as such. Procedures, which are intended to manage the vagaries of day-to-day life, have the opposite effect. They prevent us from maintaining contact with what is actually happening and from developing the necessary intelligence to make wise choices in the moment.

Process is where change hits the ground. A developmental organization grows the ability in every one of its workers to see the world in process terms. This means enabling them to be present to what is happening in this very moment. It requires that they learn to live by the principle *never do anything the same way twice*. The customer they are interacting with today is not the same person she was yesterday and not the same person she will be tomorrow. Thus, workers must learn to recognize that the process they are engaging the customer in has never happened before and will never happen again. It is particular to her in this moment and at this place. The same is true of materials, marketplaces, and even coworkers.

Building the presence of mind needed to enable everyone in an organization to make good choices from moment to moment is essential for building enduring relationships with customers. Customers are focused on what's happening in their lives right now. When a company is unable to be with them in their present, they get annoyed: "I feel like you're not listening to me!" Annoy them enough, and a business may lose them, perhaps forever. There is no place in the organization where this is not true, whether it be marketing, product design, strategic planning, or working with distribution partners. Through the products the organization offers and the services it provides, the customers recognize immediately whether the business is there with them or not.

Pretty much every business activity is a process. An activity involves a process if the word to describe it ends with -*ing*. Recruiting, interviewing, hiring, managing, disciplining, communicating, decision making, manufacturing, selling—these are all processes, regardless of how repetitive they may seem. Each person, material, or moment is unique, providing new input into the process that requires the business and its employees to be awake and present.

In phase three of work design, I make *process change* the educational focus. I invite natural working teams to transform the processes they use, and I do this in a way that evolves their ability to hold a process view of the world. As they become more self-aware, they are often shocked at how mechanical their thinking patterns are and how difficult they are to break. Teams struggle to design new processes that are consistent with the principles they have articulated and the direction in which they are trying to go. As teams test new processes in the field, they continually discover new information about how these processes actually work and the kinds of effects they produce, desirable or undesirable. Ultimately, workers learn to become sophisticated about the nature of process that will be required in any given situation.

For example, Lauri Berean is a seasonal department lead at Orchard Supply Hardware and part of a core team that I'm working with there, similar to the one we created at Seventh Generation. In one of our sessions at Orchard Supply, we explored the idea of external considering as a basis for evolving the company's approach to retail sales. Berean was inspired by the difference between having a salesperson connect with a customer's life, rather than simply ask them what they needed. Up to that point, her team had been engaging in a fairly conventional procedure: ask customers what they are looking for, their price range, and any particular specifications required. She decided to try shifting to a process orientation that sought to discover the unique circumstances customers were bringing into her store.

When I next saw her, she enthusiastically reported that she had tried it herself, working with a couple who wanted to buy a patio set and equipment to do outdoor grilling. She became their thinking partner, figuring out what kind of experience they wanted to provide for their family, how the kids would get involved, who would be coming to dinner, and so on. She and this couple were imagining together, creating a sort of shared inner movie that allowed them to see the desired grilling experience in precise detail. This helped them clarify exactly what would create their perfect garden patio. The couple was deeply grateful for the genuinely meaningful support they had received and, not coincidentally, also made a significant purchase. Later, Berean shared this with her sales team: "I finally got what it means to engage customers as unique individuals and to see the process of them living and interacting with others, rather than seeing them in terms of categories related to our products. It's so much more rewarding to interact with people this way!"

Essential Business Processes

As I mentioned earlier, the nature of the world is to change continuously, so every situation presents businesses with a new challenge. Even when the day-to-day differences seem insignificant, it is important for organizations to cultivate an attitude of wakefulness, so that they always remain relevant to what is actually occurring. The minute businesses drop into rote procedure, they lose contact with reality.

How can organizations bring this quality of wakefulness to the many processes that make up the work of a vital business? Here, for example, are some processes that most people consider essential to running an organization: hiring, working, disciplining, managing outputs, developing, and celebrating accomplishment. Because these are pretty much universal across all businesses, they get carried out in a vast number of ways. Unfortunately most of those ways have been deeply contaminated by toxic practices. In what follows, I contrast the conventional approach with a regenerative one to help you start to imagine what it might mean to evolve your organization's processes.

Hiring

Hiring is usually conducted unilaterally by an individual or a team within the company, which *buys* the services of a prospective employee based on previous achievements and ability to conform to the organization's boundaries. This symbolism is reinforced by the way in which the interview is set up, with the interviewers on one side of the table and the applicant on the other and with a one-way flow of questions. Only as an afterthought do most interviewers open space for questions from the applicant.

Hiring in a regenerative business is always reciprocal. Its purpose is to examine the potential match in a way that enables both parties to form an image of what it will be like to work together and to develop a shared aspiration to make the new relationship developmental for each. The interview will probably delve into where the company is going and the contributions it seeks to make to its stakeholders. It might also explore where in the prospective employee's work history the applicant felt most enlivened: which jobs were most meaningful. In other words, the interview is a conversation that explores for an essence-to-essence connection. This connection is an indicator that, if hired, the prospective employee will likely find ways to express his or her own potential and at the same time make an important contribution to the advancement of the company and the lives of its customers.

Working

In most companies, *working* means following a job description in order to perform tasks prescribed by others. Workers are evaluated based on their adherence to methodologies and rates of accomplishment. The implication is that the job is independent of the person filling it; it consists of a set of procedures that any qualified person should be able to follow. The main variables are the speed and accuracy with which a worker carries out the procedures. The expectation is that, with experience, an employee's performance will improve.

In a regenerative business, working is a creative process undertaken by a team. Based on the goals it has set and the strategies it is helping the business pursue, the team challenges itself to find better ways of working that will enable it to improve its effectiveness and efficiency. This collaborative process calls forth the experience of individual team members and stimulates them to pursue new achievements that will advance their professional development. Because it is not locked into pre-established procedures, a working team in a regenerative business has the freedom to invent new ways to deliver the results its customers are looking for.

Disciplining

In a conventional organization, disciplining is intended to return people to prescribed limits of behavior. It is usually conducted as a series of interventions of escalating intensity, designed to get employees' attention and measure their efforts to get themselves back within the behavioral guidelines.

Regenerative businesses avoid the need to discipline employees by helping them build self-discipline in a continuous, reciprocal process, carried out within the collegial relationships provided by working teams. Every member develops the self-discipline to help the team, and thus the business, fulfill its promises. In return, the team maintains a strong commitment to helping each member work on self-discipline. The basic instruments to enable this personal growth are behavioral principles and the capacity to be self-reflective, along with the ability to support the development of others.

Managing Outputs

A conventional business manages outputs by partitioning. Each functional group within the organization attempts independently to meet the standards and requirements of customers, while the hierarchy keeps things integrated. In many companies, this gets elaborated into the concept of "internal customers," as if by addressing the requirements of each of its divisions, the business will achieve a totality that adds up to serving external customers.

This approach sets the bar too close and too low. In a regenerative business, every team is expected to manage its work as though it was part of the customer's system. It measures its accomplishments based on the customer's outputs, not its own. In business as usual, most managers have fulfilled their responsibilities once a product has been delivered into the distribution system. In a regenerative business, teams take responsibility for effects as far downstream as they are capable of seeing. They look not only at their customers, but also at their customer's customers and beyond, seeking to produce beneficial effects for their larger communities and ecosystems.

Continuing Education

Most companies equate developing people with training them, helping them build skills they will need to perform particular functions. Some companies also work on providing challenges that will stretch their employees, giving them opportunities to grow by exposing them to diverse aspects of the business or difficult problems that need to be solved. Characteristically, these opportunities to build functional skills or breadth of experience are mandated by higher ups in the hierarchy, based on needs that management has determined. Where coaching or support is provided, it is focused on problem solving and advising, rather than on deep education to produce new, systemic thinking capacity.

In a regenerative business, educational activities are developmental. They provide resources and support as people develop the qualities they need to take charge of their own destinies and make profound contributions to their work communities. These qualities include self-management, critical-thinking skills, and the ability to embrace complexity and conflict as necessary dimensions of significant work. They are not developed accidentally, in a hit-or-miss way, and they are not grown in individuals. They are always built into the business as aspects of its culture, the ways that people work together in teams and communities. They are ritualized as regular educational events in which regenerative frameworks are used to map the dynamics of an evolving world and the work that it calls forth. And because these qualities are central to the creation of a culture of innovation, a regenerative business necessarily gives these qualities the time, attention, and investment they deserve.

Celebrating Accomplishment

Typically, businesses celebrate accomplishment at an annual event, often a dinner, where individuals who seem to have risen above the rest of their peers are singled out as role models. Superiors determine who will be selected, using competitions and awards to send strong messages about what is expected from workers by management. This approach privileges individual effort over teamwork and reinforces the narrative of the heroic individual.

In a regenerative business, accomplishment is the evolution in the capacity of a system to serve its strategic purpose. It becomes possible when a team has the courage to take on something they've never been able to figure out before (for example, ensuring on-time delivery from their customers to their customers' customers). Teams who have worked hard to create this evolution make their own decisions about the creation and timing of events at which to tell stories about their accomplishments. Storytelling is the heart of this kind of celebration. Its purpose is to strengthen the bonds within a community that has chosen to serve a common purpose.

Deer Park

When I started my work with Deer Park, a company that sells bottled spring water, it had just acquired fifty smaller businesses and become a regional brand. This was an exciting but chaotic moment. Each of these businesses had developed their own cultures and work designs, and a process to bring them together had yet to begin.

Our first task was to integrate them into a coherent company with a unified sense of identity and purpose. After all, as far as retail distributors were concerned, Deer Park was a single entity that they were prepared to trust. They would not have been happy if they encountered significant variation in the quality of service connected to the products they sold. The company needed to live up to this reasonable expectation, but this turned out to be a lot easier said than done. Many of the newly acquired businesses were located in close proximity to one another and had previously been fierce competitors in their markets. As they came together under the Deer Park label, they had to learn how to go from being near enemies to co-creators in the same business, a significant mental and emotional challenge.

We began with work on strategic direction. As a way to create a unified sense of identity, we shared the story of Deer Park's founding with representatives from all of the new businesses to discover the key images with which they resonated. It turned out that the most important of these was *clarity*. The founders of Deer Park had a strong commitment to clarity with regard to everything they did—clear water, clear bottles, clear thinking, clear communication. This became a core organizing principle for the business we were growing.

At the same time, we worked hard to shift from an internally focused and highly competitive culture to one that was concerned primarily with the criteria by which distributors measured their own success, such as shelf turnover. Following the acquisitions, Deer Park had continued to post sales results in newsletters that were circulated companywide. This exposed the sales of the former independent operators to their traditional competitors, which reinforced the impulse to compete. Teams started massaging their results in order to look good, in what felt like an environment of increasing competition. But as I began my work with them, they quickly came to see how destructive this practice was, given the new strategic direction. They decided that from that point on, the only thing they were going to measure was the success of their distributors (and by extension, the satisfaction of consumers). They made competition among themselves taboo and began reporting the results of the company as a whole.

We placed members from different businesses onto teams chartered to work together to creatively address the needs of particular customer classes. This was what we gave status to, not their previous competitive relationships. The collaborative environment was reinforced with rituals of self-development and self-reflection that enabled people to observe how their behaviors affected the success of their teams. For example, time was set aside in most meetings for teamwork on collective plans and reflections on personal self-mastery. Teams also regularly assessed how they were moving their customers' or consumers' strategies forward. It took only a year to transform what had been a collection of warring tribes into a single company entity.

As the new culture began to take hold, we set to work transforming the company's processes. For example, each hiring team turned the process into an exploration of the idea of clarity—what it meant to the company and what it meant to prospective employees. A number of people who chose to join Deer Park later reported that this conversation was decisive for them. A company that knew itself and placed high value on clarity was a refreshing change for people coming from work environments that lacked clarity of purpose, thinking, or communication.

In the first year, our development activities focused on how to create a common way of thinking that could be applied to everything Deer Park's people were working on. I introduced a limited number of powerful but accessible frameworks to generate questions that expanded and extended thinking. For example, I proposed that in every interaction, Deer Park employees were engaging in one of three modes of behavior:

- Reactive—actions dictated by external forces
- Ego driven—the source of all the problematic internal competition
- Purposeful—based on the company's commitment to serve the well-being of customers (a cause larger than themselves)

Suddenly *everyone* in the company had a common language with which to observe and manage their own behavior. This shook them up (a conscious shock!) and profoundly changed the ways they interacted within a matter of months. Instead of competing, they found themselves becoming allies and mutual teachers. The need for a common language was so important in this particular company that we immediately created a resource team dedicated to introducing this and other frameworks throughout the organization.

We also put in place a new way to celebrate the accomplishments of the various sites. Before, they had competed with one another to be recognized as "site of the month." We replaced this with a process that invited them to develop an innovation in support of distributor success and host a party when they had carried it out. The CEO required only that they offer clear justification for the celebration, based on a discernable upgrade in the customer experience.

This new practice completely changed the character of company celebrations. First of all, parties were self-organized by the sites rather than imposed from above. They became educational, as workers shared what they had accomplished with their colleagues and told stories about how they had figured it out. Buyers of their products and services were invited to attend and share stories about the accomplishment from the using end. Sometimes sites collaborated to make innovations in service of a single major customer. In one instance, they so improved the delivery system for Wegmans, a major East Coast grocery chain, that representatives from the store came to celebrate the achievement with the site, and even brought the food.

Recommendations

The invitation in phase three of work design is to explore what it takes to build the capacity for wakefulness with regard to your business processes. The point is to view the world as it actually is—alive, dynamic, in motion, and filled with opportunity for innovative action—which is only possible when you are awake. Mechanical procedures dampen creativity and erode human spirit.

You can use the essential processes I've described throughout this chapter to begin this work, but it is also important to examine your own unique business to discern the processes that are foundational for you. It is essential for you to determine how to bring the processes to life for your people, so that they become a sustaining source of energy for regenerative business practice. The following questions are intended to help you and your core team design a way to transform your business's processes by stimulating ongoing conversations and self-examination. In a regenerative business, the answers to these questions are always evolving, so the inquiry becomes ongoing.

Questions to Assess Your Business Processes

- For each of the six essential business processes described above, where does our business fall along a continuum that has a conventional approach on one end and a regenerative approach on the other? Why is it there? How have our processes improved or worsened over time?

- Are there foundational processes in our business that are not included in the list of six? How would we differentiate a conventional approach from a regenerative approach to each of these, and where are we on each continuum?

- How has this conversation affected our will to move toward a more regenerative practice?

Questions to Address the Effects of the Processes on Customers

- For each of the processes we have mapped, what is the effect of our approach on our core customers? What restraints does our approach impose on their ability to achieve their aims?

- Among these processes and their effects, where is it most critical that we begin to work to make a shift? What change(s) would produce the most leveraged impact?

- Who needs to be invested in this change if it is to be successful?

Questions to Address Growing a Companywide Process Orientation

- How do we educate our peers throughout the organization by engaging them in the same assessment and will-building dialogue?

- Where do less-than-regenerative organizational patterns show up in our team? In our work as individuals? How will we engage other teams and all individuals in our organization in their own assessments?

- How do we keep this conversation alive so that we can help one another make the shifts that we see are needed? What agreements do we want to make in order to support each individual's efforts to stay awake?

CHAPTER TEN

Phase Four—Evolve Business Work Systems

Systems are means for managing and improving the effectiveness of the value-adding process in serving its purpose by matching patterns in a dynamic world, not ways to control behavior.

Charles Krone, Visionary Chemical Engineer, Procter and Gamble
Business Designer

ONCE A COMPANY has charted a new strategic direction for itself, started to grow a new culture, and transformed its key processes, it will no longer fit comfortably in its own skin. At this point, it will need to redesign its systems and structures to better serve the role it has chosen to play in its market and industry.

Five Phases of Innovative Work Disruption

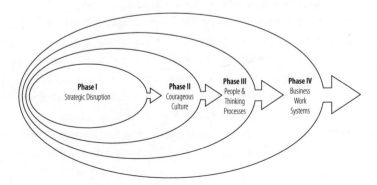

Organizations create systems to keep multiple people and functions aligned, so that they can achieve a shared purpose in a relatively predictable way. Systems help keep regularly recurring activities, such as payroll and invoicing, well organized and orderly. They maintain continuity, allowing businesses to remain in integrity with the culture and direction they are pursuing.

Systems become anti-developmental when they drive organizations' decisions rather than serve the decision-making processes. This happens when people use them to replace the need for thinking about something. For example, a forecasting system predicts sales, which determines production, which anticipates returns, which drives stock values. Such a system can usefully expedite the calculation of all of these variables, but it will fall apart if people don't exercise the discipline to regularly think about, challenge, and upgrade the assumptions around which it has been built.

For a company that aims to be developmental, the appropriate design of systems becomes very important. On the one hand, organizations want them to have the effect of continually fostering innovation across the company, in every worker. On the other, businesses rely on them to provide the boundaries and organizing principles that allow these innovations to remain aligned and coherent. In a regenerative organization, systems themselves are instruments for the development of people—designed to be managed and continuously upgraded by those who are using them, rather than by outside experts.

One of the reasons that so many of the systems found in businesses work against innovation is that they are intended to make things easy, rather than make them developmental. For example, many companies install internal accounting systems that measure the expenses of individual units, which inadvertently and inappropriately focus attention on the need to compete within the company. An innovation-supporting accounting system assesses performance of the company as a whole, based on improvements in how customers measure their successes.

Typical business systems are designed by experts as packages that serve a particular function and can then be shoehorned into an organization.

By definition, these systems are neither integrated with one another nor indigenous to the organization's culture. As a result, they require ongoing maintenance from the outside experts who created them.

According to my mentor, Charles Krone, developmental organizations use systems to engage in *value-adding processes*. For Krone, a value-adding process works simultaneously on improving product offerings, improving the methods of production, and improving the capabilities of everyone involved. Toward this end, he described five critical categories of organizational systems: managing, operating, personnel, site, and planning.[1]

Taken together, these systems provide both the freedom and the order needed for people to engage their personal agency with regard to serving their customers. One key characteristic of a developmental organization is that its systems are designed to resource workers as they evolve themselves on the job, supported by ongoing education that develops their thinking capabilities and grows them as people. In other words, workers learn to engage with systems proactively, so that even as they use them they are able to understand and critically challenge them for the purpose of upgrading their intentions and effects. For each of Krone's five categories of system, this means developing a particular capability across the entire workforce.

Here I look at each category of system in more detail and give some real-world examples.

Managing

Managing systems work on increasing the value generated in reciprocal exchange with the external world. At every customer interface, managing systems should ensure total satisfaction.

> *Amazon, for example, has become dominant in its market by setting up systems designed to consistently give purchasers an experience of customized service, without their ever having direct contact with employees. On the relatively rare occasions when things go wrong, it's easy for customers to reach live service agents.[2]*

By increasing the value of its offerings, a company increases the value that its beneficiaries have available for use, and this is reciprocated in such forms as increased loyalty and willingness to pay higher margins. To accomplish this, workers must develop the capability to imagine the effects that will ripple out from each of their actions. Instead of taking for granted the appropriateness of activities prescribed by a system, they are able to assess the consequences of those activities on stakeholders and thereby improve the system.

> *An Amazon employee recently set out to radically reduce the amount of packaging involved in delivering products through the mail, one of the persistent weaknesses in the company's customer interface.*

Site

Site systems work on the interacting dynamic flows—for example, of material, equipment, and people—required for operational work. Developmental organizations begin by growing consciousness of those flows in order to manage their movement and interactions. Regenerative businesses then evolve the flows to remove wasted effort and to enable more effective, flexible operations.

> *The engineering design team at Google did some deep thinking about the ways people would move through its platforms and, based on what they learned, designed their search engine for optimal successful use. One probability that struck the team early on was that a high percentage of search terms would be misspelled. Thus, they created systems that would offer alternate spellings as a way to make almost every search foolproof.*

The critical capability needed for designing and improving site systems has to do with letting go of what currently exists—including all of the limitations built in to the ways that the various elements of the business currently work—in order to see directly into how things *want* to work. This is the hallmark of innovative designers and architects, who free themselves from existing expectations of how things *should* work in order to discover how they *could* work.

Operating

Operating systems work to improve performance across various aspects of an organization in order to build its overall effectiveness at producing intended results. Thus, they focus on the way work gets done.

> Southwest Airlines built its business model around flying only one kind of airplane, the Boeing 737, so that every plane and every part is interchangeable, and every mechanic, pilot, and member of the cabin crews knows all of the planes they're responsible for intimately.[3]

Because a developmental organization is never self-referential, operating systems also need to take into account exactly the results that are expected from a product when a customer uses it. Instead of merely measuring internal output, a regenerative business measures what is most significant in terms of producing the customer's desired outcomes. It asks, "How is what *we* are doing changing what *they* are able to do?"

> By limiting itself to one kind of plane, Southwest has been able to deliver high levels of safety and on-time arrival for passengers.

To provide benefits that meet or exceed customer expectations, workers must learn to shift identity, conceiving of themselves as if they were in their customers' shoes, on their team, working with them as a cocreators. In this way, they make themselves champions of their customers' success.

Personnel

Personnel systems work on growing people as a way to evolve the development and expression of an organization's potential within the context of agreed upon purposes.

> In a regenerative organization, systems are designed to call on people to propose their own work—much as Google requires its employees to discover their roles within the organization by discerning what's needed.

This is fundamentally unlike the conventional system of job descriptions, which is designed to slot people into existing, predetermined positions. A company that wants to access the potential of its employees creates a way for them to accurately identify the strategic opportunities that will make a better business. Pursuing these opportunities provides the ground for employees to chart developmental paths for themselves, paths that will also advance the company's strategic direction. Over time, they build the experiential base to take on challenges of increasing scope and complexity.

> *This is partly the rationale for Google's famous practice of allowing its engineers to dedicate 20 percent of their time to innovations that go beyond their regular work focus.*[4]

Planning

Planning systems lay out the work that needs to be done and then ensure that production stays on track with regard to strategy, budget, and goals. In the most sophisticated systems, planning means more than just auditing to be sure the organization is doing what it said it was going to do, on time and in budget. It also means evaluating whether or not the business is creating results that will deliver the profound qualitative improvement in the lives of customers that the organization envisioned in phase one.

> *Orchard Supply Hardware has differentiated itself from larger big box chains not only by supplying more of what customers need, but also by anticipating what customers are going to need in the future, based on local neighborhood conditions.*

It's not enough to check off boxes with regard to goals and benchmarks. Collectively, the entire organization needs to be continually evaluating whether those goals and benchmarks are actually making a difference. Are products and services getting better all the time? This requires growing the people within the organization, and thus the planning team must also check to be sure that every department has a plan for developing its people as they do their work.

In a recent meeting, Orchard Supply's core team realized that it could do more to fulfill its commitment to anticipate customers' needs and committed itself to a complete overhaul of its inventory systems.

As a company's strategy evolves, its systems should evolve as well. In a regenerative business, people within the organization take this on, and it becomes a critical arena for their personal and professional development, forming a basis for their promises beyond ableness. Typically, employees dedicate a couple of years' work to improving one system before moving on to tackle another, bringing the proficiency they've acquired with them. With each new design challenge, employees push themselves to find increasingly elegant solutions for managing more and more complex dynamics. This keeps the work fresh and inspiring, and over time it allows everyone an opportunity to contribute to the evolution of every system in the business.

A change in systems is triggered by an evolution of strategy, but unlike the introduction of new processes, system change is slower, deeper, and takes more effort. It also builds greater longevity into the change process, as systems reflect and reinforce the regenerative approach that is beginning to take root.

Colgate, Salford, England

I met Whitcomb Roberts at Colgate's production facility in Salford, England, where he was a new hire working on a line in the deodorant unit. Over the years I knew him, Roberts demonstrated a real gift for systems evolution. He attributed this to his upbringing on a farm, where in order to stay in business, his family paid constant attention to how all systems were integrated. As he put it, "You had to be pervasive in your actions." At Colgate, nothing annoyed him more than noticing when something critical was not pervasively adopted.

Like other new hires, Roberts was required to spend his first year studying the systems he was interacting with in order to see how they worked and to notice where they were breaking down. At the end of his year, he pointed out that there seemed to be no connection between what was happening in his business unit and the overall corporate direction that Colgate Europe had set for itself. This made no sense to him. Colgate Europe had committed to becoming an integrated company across all of the countries within the European Union, and he had been told at his orientation that this would guide both his own actions and the actions of his team. Yet he could find little evidence that this was actually happening.

Consequently, Roberts decided to work on this aspect of managing systems, and he set out to experiment. At first he simply talked to his coworkers about what they were doing and how it connected to integrating all of Colgate's European plants. That didn't go very far. Then he tried creating a brief newsletter that would share stories about where people were trying to address unification. But this also frustrated him, because it was episodic and not very effective. He realized that he needed to find a way to systematize attention to the subject.

Finally, he hit on the idea of introducing the subject of integration into the existing reporting systems across the facility. Each business unit was already required to do a quarterly report on its production. Into this matrix, he inserted a section that asked for a report on what they had done to advance the integration process.

This turned out to be significant because Colgate had such a strong history of competition among its various European branches. Each had started out producing the entire line of Colgate products, and thus they often found themselves competing among themselves for the same distribution channels. As the company worked on European unification, it began to sort the production of different product lines among different countries.

Roberts' simple question invited his colleagues to ask how they could begin to cooperate with other plants across Europe to facilitate this change. It was so successful at Salford that it was soon adopted by business units across Europe, and it was included in every aspect of reporting. This fostered a new spirit of shared information and coordination.

Roberts had successfully completed the first stage of his developmental work plan and was ready to tackle a more complex system. He attended one of the meetings that the Salford business periodically hosted to help employees transition to their next level of challenge. During that meeting, he learned about the work that the core team had been doing to identify the company's core buyer nodes.

This resonated deeply with him. He told the core team that as a hobby, he had spent much of his life carving small, traditional musical instruments—whistles and flutes—and that he had custom made every one of them for the person who would play it. The idea of workers putting themselves in the shoes of the buyer made perfect sense to him, but he could see that it would also be a big challenge to make this practice pervasive across all two thousand employees at Salford. This, he decided, was a challenge he wanted to take on. It would require him to focus on operating systems.

Roberts was a Yorkshireman, a natural storyteller, and he knew instinctively that no amount of demographic information was going to help his fellow workers feel a strong connection to the people whom they were serving. What was needed, he believed, were stories and a way to get these stories told to every operational team in every department. He tapped into an existing system that had been established to feed demographics gathered by the marketing team into the weekly meetings held by work teams. By changing what marketing was delivering from dry statistics to stories about real consumers, he was able to introduce a strong sense of human connection into every team in the facility every week.

This approach began to stimulate conversations within and among teams about what would be required to upgrade buyers' experiences. For example, the storytelling rituals fostered an extended dialogue among marketing, researchers, and line operators—including young people for whom this was a first job—about how to create a breakthrough innovation in oral health products. As they explored what life was like for consumers, especially for busy young families, they could see that a single product that strengthened teeth, protected gums, and prevented bad breath would simplify people's daily regimens. Picked up and developed by Colgate's U.S. labs, this seed idea became Total Toothpaste, the number one brand in Europe within a few years of its introduction.

Roberts was soon promoted, and very quickly he saw that his new position of supervisor, as it was currently defined, was undermining the

creative self-accountability that had enabled his own rise in the organization. He saw that the company needed to help supervisors transition from
overseeing and directing people to helping them radically improve business processes. Work teams were rapidly learning to manage themselves
and no longer needed management from above. Roberts decided to help
supervisors become resources and advisors to these teams.

Inspired by the potential he saw in some experiments that were under
way in Colgate's plant in Greece, he set out to redefine the supervisor role
and build a system that would enable Salford's supervisors to make the
transition. He recognized the accumulated experience and wisdom of this
group. Whereas other companies frequently dismiss managers in their
efforts to create flatter organizations, he sought an unthreatening way to
elevate the use of the supervisors' talents.

Roberts began by writing a report that summarized the experiments
in Greece and their larger implications. This built confidence that what he
wanted to do could work. Then he gathered supervisors from across the
organization, explained the project, and invited them to think about the
arenas that most interested them and to which they could make the greatest contribution. For example, a couple of supervisors were particularly
good at helping teams build the skills they needed to be self-managing,
while another supervisor had a special talent for understanding machinery
and how it could be adapted to serve new purposes. By the time each had
weighed in, they had covered nearly all of the capabilities that the plant
would need to launch a culture of team-based innovation.

Out of this, Roberts was able to build a system within which every
supervisor would play a dual role. Each would work closely with several
teams as a resource to decision making and implementation, and at the
same time each would bring his or her special expertise to any Salford
teams that required it. Roberts set up ongoing training for the supervisors
so that they could improve their abilities to play these roles.

Roberts realized that his proposed changes represented a radical break
from Colgate's traditional culture of top-down delegation. Although they
were consistent with the new course the company was charting, they were
likely to encounter resistance from outside of Salford. To address this
concern, he recruited a team of top leaders at Salford, as well as members

from Colgate's headquarters in Brussels, to serve as advisors and champions for his effort. He wanted these leaders to be up to speed on what he was doing and help him avoid major blunders, but he also wanted them to serve as an umbrella that would protect his fragile experiment, giving it time to prove itself.

It's important to note that individuals do not undertake a change process like this on their own. Roberts identified a strategic opportunity to upgrade a personnel system and made a promise beyond ableness to bring together a team to work on it. About ten people responded to his invitation, and together they made it happen. Roberts served as leader, not boss, and reflected in his own person the qualities he was trying to support systemically across the company. The overwhelming success of his efforts came to the attention of many other teams in Europe and awakened the desire in a number of emerging leaders to try their hand at addressing the same questions. This ultimately led to Roberts' invitation to join the corporate leadership team in Brussels.

Recommendations

Although the questions that follow are intended to help you think about and work on evolving the systems in your organization, I strongly recommend that you wait to answer them until you have already done significant work in the prior three phases. Your answers need to come from experience that you have built through a committed change process. How is this affecting performance? Your position within the market? The spirit of your people? Only when you can base your answers on concrete experience are you really in a position to move forward with changing systems and structures. Given this caveat, here are questions to help you think about systems evolution.

Questions to Identify the Systems that Need to Be Established or Evolved

- Using the five categories of system—managing, operating, personnel, site, and planning—as an organizing framework, which of our recurring activities need to be systemized in ways that are developmental if we are to continue evolving as a regenerative organization?

- Which systems are already in place? How will they need to be evolved if they are to support the regenerative direction we are pursuing?

- Are there missing systems that we will need to create?

Questions to Identify which Systems Actually Restrain Growth and Potential

- Among the systems that we currently have in place, which need immediate attention and a complete overhaul because they are based on toxic practices?

- What principles should guide the way we redesign our systems so that their original purposes are fulfilled, even as we make them more workable and developmental?

- What processes do we need to embed in our systems so that they are continuously re-examined, refreshed, and made relevant?

Questions to Address the Need to Engage the Entire Organization

- Where is the most highly leverageable place to begin work on systems change?

- What can be done at the team level, and what needs to be businesswide?

- How do we create an effective campaign to meaningfully connect people to the shifts in systems that we are seeking?

CHAPTER ELEVEN

Phase Five—Evolve Work Structures *Last*

Critical thinking is thinking about your thinking while you're thinking in order to make your thinking better.

Richard W. Paul, Founder of the Center for Critical Thinking

STRUCTURES ARE USEFUL whenever an entity needs stability. Structures serve as the enduring frame within which change happens, providing the coherence that allows an entity to grow and evolve without descending into chaos. In many contexts, structures remain relatively static, even as people or flows move through them. For example, streets and highways lay down a basic grid through which traffic flows and around which other structures are situated, such as buildings and parks.

Work design also uses structures to direct traffic, but in this case traffic is the ingenuity and decision making required to get work done. In a regenerative organization, work design produces dynamic stability, like the stability required to ride a bicycle or ski down a mountain, and its structures support evolution rather than stasis.

Five Phases of Innovative Work Disruption

Structures dictate choices and cannot be shifted or removed without real investment of effort. Once they are in place, they tend to encourage some options and prohibit others. For example, when a builder has finished framing in a kitchen, it's difficult or prohibitively expensive to turn it into a bedroom. At the same time, if structures aren't designed to respect the reality of critical processes, then people tend to ignore them. For example, college students famously refuse to keep off the grass when sidewalks don't take them directly to where they are trying to go.

In most organizations, structures show up as hierarchies, roles, job descriptions, teams, pay and progression programs, procedures for information sharing, and behavior management. In a developmental organization, the challenge is to create structures that are durable and reliable yet designed to foster flexibility and growth. This is accomplished by reducing dependence on rigid or material structures and instituting higher-order, conceptual structures.

Three Kinds of Regenerative Structure

Based on my experience over the past four decades, I propose the development of three kinds of structure that can support the evolution of a regenerative business:

- Developmental thinking structures
- Generative structures
- Manifestation structures

Developmental Thinking Structures

Thinking structures shape and direct our mental processes. For example, businesses will use cost-benefit analyses to organize their thinking about where to invest. As often as not, we utilize thinking structures without awareness of them, and they function as mental models. That is, they nudge us into predetermined patterns of thought. A particularly insidious example of this kind of mental model is the habit of unconsciously dividing people into "us" and "them."

Developmental thinking structures, on the other hand, enable us to become conscious of the way our thinking is structured and to reshape it. The frameworks offered in this book are a good example. Whereas mental models channel thinking along familiar paths, frameworks cause us to extend the depth and complexity of our thinking and the difficulty of the challenges we take on. This opens us to genuinely innovative insights.

For example, we may unconsciously experience the world as polarized—right or wrong, winner or loser, left wing or right wing—a framing that may have formed in our minds early on, reinforced by parents, church, or social milieu. When we are faced with a challenging decision, the unconscious mental structure of polarity limits the options that appear to be available to us. To broaden our options, we can use a developmental thinking structure to actively examine the decision. We might ask ourselves, "Where is the complementarity in this situation? How might I reconcile these seemingly contradictory options or points of view?" However, this is only possible if we become aware of the fact that our original thinking was structured by the idea of polarity.

Introducing developmental thinking structures is one way for organizations to enable the work of the previous four phases of regenerative work design. By using developmental thinking structures to break outworn thinking habits and replace them with flexible practices that are consistent with the dynamics of a changing world, businesses open the door to new organizational direction, culture, processes, and systems. More importantly, they create the conditions to make a real difference in the world.

Developmental thinking structures that I have already introduced in this book are the Criteria for Growing Human Capacity (chapter 3) and the Conditions for Enlightened Disruption (chapter 4). All of the structures that I will describe in this chapter flow from and are informed by these.

Generative Structures

Generative structures enable a company to transform itself from functionally static to functionally dynamic by disrupting familiar ways of working that have become calcified, dysfunctional, or outdated. In most of the organizations I've worked with, I've introduced a *core team/market field team/task team* structure to accomplish this disruption. It has been my preferred way to initiate phase one of an organizational change process.

The *core team* is chartered to understand the dynamic world it inhabits in order to strategically position and internally develop its business to produce the most meaningful impacts possible. For this reason, a core team needs to reflect all of the relevant perspectives of the organization's members and stakeholders so that the intelligence of the entire organization is present in the room. It must also include people with the authority to make fiduciary decisions, enabling it to quickly implement its strategies. Consequently, core teams often turn out to be cross-functional and multilevel, and their dialogues are correspondingly rich.

A core team identifies critical work that has been ignored, such as discovering the essence of buyers, and it democratizes work that has formerly been the province of small groups, such as marketing or tracking financial performance. At the same time, it evolves work design in ways that generate new capacity. One of a core team's key responsibilities is to sustain its ability to disrupt existing patterns so that the organization can sustain its ability to evolve.

Market field teams dedicate themselves to understanding customers, whose choices determine whether a company will remain in business. Each team focuses on a specific buyer class, inquiring deeply into its unique needs and aspirations. This generates a strong sense of connection and provides the basis for designing the innovations that will produce beneficial effects in customers' lives. It also disrupts the compartmentalized processes by which new products and services are usually created. The market field teams receive support and take strategic direction from the core team.

From time to time, the strategic growth of an organization requires focused work to develop new systems or processes. This is the role of *task teams*, whose scope is always clearly defined and whose members disband once their work is accomplished. Because task teams serve the transformation of particular aspects of the business, they are inherently formed to serve disruptive purposes.

Manifestation Structures

Manifestation structures direct the flow of decisions, outcomes, and accountability so that the daily cycle of work can get done. Business leaders who have made a promise to their board or investors need to know that their commitment will be translated throughout the company. They need to establish some level of control that lets them know that their people are making appropriate decisions for which they will be held accountable. Traditional manifestation structures, such as hierarchies or job descriptions, are intended to serve this purpose.

In a regenerative organization, workers are expected to be self-motivating, self-managing, and conscious of the whole of the business, as created and held by its strategic direction; the essence and identity of buyer classes and how they live; financial performance; primary processes, systems, and structures; and so forth. Because it starts from this philosophy, a regenerative organization designs very different manifestation structures than are usually found in a conventional business. Here are some examples.

- In conventional reporting structures, higher levels in a hierarchy provide to lower levels their plans, procedures, and standards, ensuring compliance in order to obtain orderly, controlled operations and improvements. In contrast, a regenerative reporting structure expects that levels are needed only in order to provide a distinctive and additive contribution toward business and functional excellence. No one serves as boss over another person's work. In some instances, supervisors might become educators, providing expertise to help teams achieve the purposes they undertake on behalf of the business. In other cases, they may resource an employee's personal development. Roles will evolve as the company evolves.

- Conventional work allocation structures almost always take the form of job descriptions, which delineate specific tasks and work focus. A regenerative structure takes the form of self-defined roles for every employee—such as *champion for improving communications between sales and production*—that address some important business need or opportunity. Roles are self-initiated, unrelated or only indirectly related to an employee's usual work, and temporary. This fosters the flexibility required to carry out operations, even as employees grow new capabilities by taking on increasingly challenging roles. For example, David Thau, an engineer at Google, decided to find a way to map deforestation in the Amazon. He defined his role and its outcomes, sought the help he needed, and worked to accomplish the task, while at the same time responsibly managing his engineering work.[1]

- Conventional pay structures are based on seniority and the completion of training and experience for a particular job. Regenerative pay structures are based on the successful development and application of new capabilities to mutually agreed upon activities that are designed to improve the business. As employees take on increasingly challenging and comprehensive improvements, their pay increases correspondingly.

- Within conventional organizations, team structures are usually built around shared responsibility for a particular kind of work, such as marketing. Occasionally, leadership will set up cross-functional teams to carry out a particular task, such as acquiring new operating systems. Although functional teams are a part of a regenerative organization, a far more important structure is made up of teams that organize themselves around serving specific customers. The outward orientation of these teams draws people together from across the organization. It connects them personally to the market, and it gives them an experience of the relationships among their different roles within the unified company.

• Conventional behavior management structures are set up to communicate standards and exercise control by taking progressive action against those who don't conform to definitions of acceptable behavior. These actions can readily transition into assembling the dreaded "file," a euphemism for building a case for firing someone.

In a regenerative organization, individuals and teams are accountable for their behavior based on mutually agreed upon principles and purposes. This works because teams create clear deliverables linked to the markets they serve and because self-reflection is built into every team process. Also, resourcing support is made continuously available rather than provided only during annual reviews.

W. L. Gore & Associates

Bill Gore, the inventor of Gore-Tex, never pulled his punches when it came to how much he had hated working at DuPont as a young chemical engineer. He hated getting someone else's approval for everything he wanted to do; he hated working through strict channels of communication; and he hated being thwarted when it came to following up on his creative ideas. It's not surprising, then, that in 1958 he left DuPont to found his own company. Within two years, W. L. Gore & Associates had introduced revolutionary product innovations for surgery, firefighting, and outdoor sports.

During his time at DuPont, Gore met my colleague James V. Clark. In 1960, Clark invited Gore to a consortium that was hosted by UCLA's Institute for Labor and Employment. The consortium featured forward-thinking companies like Procter & Gamble, Honda, Sherwin Williams, and Tektronix.

This experience was a watershed moment for Gore. He came home with a clear image of a completely new kind of company, structured as what he would later call a *lattice organization*. In his conceptualization, the entire business would function like one big team. There would be no bosses. There would be no channels of communication; all communication would be direct. And anyone could initiate work to improve the safety and performance of their products.

Instead of bosses, W. L. Gore & Associates adopted the idea of *sponsors*, people who had direct experience in a field—for example, from having visited and observed work in an operating room—and a clear picture of the improvements that could serve it. It was up to sponsors to persuade their colleagues to form a team with them, but if enough people were willing, they could go directly to work on manifesting their ideas. The only caveat was that none of these projects could fall "below the waterline," that is, pose an existential risk to the company. To take on *that* level of risk required agreement from across the entire organization.

W. L. Gore & Associates also pioneered the title of *associate* for every member of the company. Because everyone was equal, associates were expected to communicate directly with any other associates who were likely to be affected by innovations they were stewarding. In this ever-changing organization, communications were highly fluid and based on what was most needed for the work at hand. (This is still true today.)

The looseness of this structure, without hierarchy, decision-making controls, or accountability oversight, may seem counterintuitive. But it is precisely why W. L. Gore & Associates was quickly able to become a global company, why it has remained resistant to recession through sixty years of repeated up and down cycles, and why it continues to be a leader in financial growth within its industry.

Recommendations

Structuring is intimately tied to the way you have answered the questions and implemented changes in all of the earlier phases, so I cannot offer you specific recommendations to structure your business in a new way. However, in the spirit of open inquiry, I will close with a few general questions for your consideration. By the time you get to this phase in your organizational change process, you will also be able to develop your own questions.

- *Among the ideas that have been presented in this chapter, are there any that particularly excite you or seem to have the potential to create significant benefit for your business?*
- *On the other hand, which of these ideas scare the hell out of you? Why?* Paying attention to what unsettles you is a great way to understand the potential for real change.
- *What education is your organization prepared to get started on now—and how can you use the supplemental materials associated with this book to help it get started?* None of the structural changes proposed here will be successful or meaningful unless they are paired with education and human development. Don't experiment in the structural arena; experiment with education.

Free download: Supplemental materials to help start your business's regenerative work design at *www.CarolSanford.com/bookdownloads*.

Epilogue: The Regenerative Paradigm

The essence of the independent mind lies not in what it thinks, but in how it thinks.

Christopher Hitchens, *Letters to a Young Contrarian*

A T THE END OF CHAPTER 2 I introduced six current and pressing issues that business executives are focused on these days and that I get asked about all the time: hiring and retaining talent, becoming a best place to work, making a company an innovation powerhouse, building resilience to weather wild fluctuation in markets, dealing with ever-increasing complexity, and making a company a healthy place to work. At this point in the book, I hope that it's become clear how a regenerative approach addresses all of these simultaneously, as the byproduct of creating an innovative company. In a regenerative business, these issues simply become irrelevant.

A regenerative business doesn't get into bidding wars for talent because it grows its own. It doesn't need to chase after trendy benefits packages because it attracts and keeps people by offering them profoundly meaningful work to do. Innovation isn't isolated in research and development labs because it has become the responsibility of everyone in the company. A regenerative business can manage wild fluctuations in the market because it works on the resilience and agility of its people through the ways that it designs, manages, and conducts work. Managing complexity is no longer an executive suite problem because everyone is trained in the collective use of systemic frameworks. And the best way to keep people healthy and happy is to provide them with opportunities to express their potential in service to something greater than themselves.

In other words, a regenerative approach to work design is elegant. It simply dissolves the kinds of issues that cause other executives to tear their hair out. It does this by giving workers permission to focus on potential rather than problems and, thereby, to create the world that wants to come into existence.

Where to Begin

The changes I'm advocating might seem daunting, even overwhelming. I certainly intend them to be comprehensive. It would be perfectly natural for a reader to wonder where and how to begin.

Early in chapter 2 I described three paradigms—*performance improvement*, *human growth*, and *systems regeneration*—that inform three very different approaches to work design. The most direct and immediately available first step to building a regenerative business is to become aware of the paradigms that lie behind its decisions and actions, and to evolve those paradigms.

A business that sees people as basically fixed and unchangeable can investigate this belief and start to explore the possibility that any person can grow and change. A business that already recognizes the innate potential of human beings can extend its horizons to see that self-actualization, in the long run, is far less satisfying than systems actualizing, Truly developmental organizations provide the context for individuals to become contributing members of a larger community and to grow themselves in order to serve a purpose that they deem worthy.

Evolving the paradigms that shape your own thinking and the thinking of your business's people is something that you can do as an individual, beginning today if you choose. But it becomes far more powerful and far easier to sustain when you do it with a community. For example, you could gather a group of your colleagues to read and discuss this book and the ideas it raises.

Democracy Requires a New Workplace

Finally, I want to enlarge on a theme that I believe is particularly important and also easy to overlook. Throughout all the chapters of this book, I've hinted at one of the compelling motivations I had for writing it. I believe that businesses, beyond their drive to succeed and to improve life for their customers, play a pivotal role in determining the health of democracies. Yes, I want to see individual businesses and employees flourish. But I'm equally concerned by what I see as an erosion of democratic institutions in the world.

The very same activities that make a business a transformative leader in its industry will also build an engaged citizenry. Developing *internal locus of control* is central to becoming responsible adults with the independence of mind to question received wisdom—including the supposed wisdom of our social networks. Without this capability, voters give away their right to make sound decisions based on their own reasoned opinions.

At the same time, internal locus of control can become inhumane and self-justifying when it isn't linked to and balanced by *external considering*, which always seeks to understand what life is like for those who are different from us. Much of our political discourse reflects a rift between these two perspectives, even though they are necessary complements to one another. Some political leaders argue for the importance of standing on one's own two feet and taking responsibility for one's life. Absolutely true. Others argue for the social necessity and benefit of caring for the entire body politic, young or old, weak or strong, native or immigrant. Also absolutely true.

As I hope I've demonstrated in this book, business is the place where these supposedly contradictory requirements can be reconciled, so long as we've created businesses that develop the full human capacity of their workers. And for a participatory democracy, as for an innovative company, *personal agency* is where citizenship hits the ground. It's not enough to sit in front of our laptops and complain about the decisions others are making on our behalf. A democracy lives or dies based on the full engagement of its members.

When I worked with Colgate in South Africa during the country's transition from apartheid, workers were immediately translating what they were learning to organizing the emerging governance of their townships. Literally—they were applying lessons learned the very same day. There was no question in their minds that they needed to exercise internal locus of control, external considering, and personal agency. Their future and the future of their country depended on it, and their company was giving them the opportunity they needed to find their wings and take flight.

Democracy is fragile, and more so now in our technological age than ever before. A democratic nation depends upon the will and caring of its people if it is to endure. But if we are inattentive, this will and caring can be degraded or destroyed by institutions of business, education, and governance that replace human creativity with systems of manipulation and control. This is why I believe so deeply that the renewal of democratic institutions depends on growing the innovative capacity of businesses. And this is one reason why I have written this book—as an invitation to businesses and businesspeople who want to take on this important work around the world.

Notes

Introduction

1. Curtis Sittenfeld, "Powered by the People," *Fast Company* (December 19, 2007), accessed March 25, 2017, www.fastcompany.com/37301/powered-people.

Chapter 1

1. Alfred R. Mele, "Motivation and Agency," Oxford Scholarship Online (November 2003), accessed March 25, 2017, www.oxfordscholarship.com/view/10.1093/019515617X.001.0001/acprof-9780195156171.
2. Theodore A. Walls and Todd D. Little, "Relations Among Personal Agency, Motivation, and School Adjustment in Early Adolescence," *Journal of Educational Psychology* 97, no. 1 (2005): 23–32.
3. Daphne Brandenburg, "Implicit Attitudes and the Social Capacity for Free Will," *Philosophical Psychology* 29, no. 8 (August 2016), accessed March 25, 2017, www.tandfonline.com/doi/full/10.1080/09515089.2016.1235263.
4. Andrea Lavazza, "Free Will and Neuroscience: From Explaining Freedom Away to New Ways of Operationalizing and Measuring It," *Frontiers of Human Neuroscience* (June 1, 2016), accessed March 25, 2017, http://journal.frontiersin.org/article/10.3389/fnhum.2016.00262/full.
5. Patrick Frick and Chris Luebkeman, "Planet-Centered Design: A Mindset Shift for Engaging Complexity," *Huffington Post* (January 24, 2017), accessed March 25, 2017, http://www.huffingtonpost.com/entry/planet-centred-design-a-mind-set-shift-for-engaging_us_587fa87ce4b06a0baf64924e.
6. "Special Report on Artificial Intelligence: The Impact on Jobs—Automation and Agency," *The Economist* (June 25, 2016), accessed March 25, 2017, www.economist.com/news/special-report/21700758-will-smarter-machines-cause-mass-unemployment-automation-and-anxiety.
7. Quincy Larson, "A Warning from Elon Musk, Bill Gates, and Stephen Hawking," freeCodeCamp, accessed March 13, 2017, https://medium.

freecodecamp.org/bill-gates-and-elon-musk-just-warned-us-about-the-one-thing-politicians-are-too-scared-to-talk-8db9815fd398.

8. Patreese D. Ingram, "The Ups and Downs of the Workplace," *Journal of Extension* 44, no. 3 (June 2006), accessed March 25, 2017, https://joe.org/joe/2006june/comm1.php.

9. D'Vera Cohn and Andrea Caumont, "10 Demographic Trends that Are Shaping the U.S. and the World," Pew Research Center Fact Tank (March 31, 2016), accessed March 25, 2017, www.pewresearch.org/fact-tank/2016/03/31/10-demographic-trends-that-are-shaping-the-u-s-and-the-world.

10. Carol Sanford, *The Responsible Business: Reimagining Sustainability and Success* (San Francisco: Jossey-Bass, 2011).

11. Quincy Larson, "A Warning from Elon Musk."

Chapter 2

1. For more about sustainability and regeneration: Pamela Mang, Ben Haggard, and Regenesis, *Regenerative Development and Design* (Hoboken, New Jersey: John Wiley & Sons, Inc., 2016).

2. Carol S. Dweck, *Mindset: The New Psychology of Business* (New York: Random House, 2016).

3. Tim Kastelle, "Hierarchy Is Overrated," *Harvard Business Review* (November 20, 2013), accessed March 25, 2017, https://hbr.org/2013/11/hierarchy-is-overrated.

4. Jeffrey G. Covin and Dennis P. Slevin, "The Influence of Organization Structure on the Utility of an Entrepreneurial Top Management Style," *Journal of Management Studies* 25, no. 3 (May 1988): 217–234, accessed March 25, 2017, http://onlinelibrary.wiley.com/doi/10.1111/j.1467-6486.1988.tb00033.x/abstract.

5. George Meszaros, "What Percentage of Businesses Fail?" *Success Harbor* (April 21, 2016), accessed March 25, 2017, www.successharbor.com/percentage-businesses-fail-09092015.

6. Douglas A. Ready, Linda A. Hill, and Jay A. Conger, "Winning the Race for Talent in Emerging Markets," *Harvard Business Review* (November 2008): Reprint: R0811C, accessed March 25, 2017, https://hbr.org/2008/11/winning-the-race-for-talent-in-emerging-markets.

7. PwC (member firms of PricewaterhouseCoopers International Limited), "14th Annual Global CEO Survey" (2011), accessed March 25, 2017, www.pwc.com/gx/en/hr-management-services/assets/ceo-survey-talent-race.pdf.

8. Matthew A. Cole and Eric Neumayer, "The Impact of Poor Health on Factor Productivity: An Empirical Investigation," *Journal of Development Studies* 42, no. 6 (2006): 918–938, accessed March 25, 2017, http://eprints .lse.ac.uk/19780/1/The%20impact%20of%20poor%20health%20on% 20factor%20productivity(lseror).pdf.

9. Emile Tompa, "The Impact of Health on Productivity: Empirical Evidence and Policy Implications," *The Review of Economic Performance and Social Progress* (2002), accessed March 25, 2017, www.csls.ca/repsp/2/emiletompa .pdf.

10. Emma Seppala and Kim Cameron, "Proof that Positive Work Environments are More Productive," *Harvard Business Review* (December 1, 2015), accessed March 25, 2017, https://hbr.org/2015/12/proof-that-positive -work-cultures-are-more-productive.

Chapter 3

1. Teuta Zogaj and Toni Didona, "The Effects of Self-Esteem and Locus of Control on Work Productivity," *International Journal of Business and Management Studies* 1 (2012): 3, accessed March 25, 2017, http://universitypublications .net/ijbms/0103/html/HVD238.xml.

2. Khiv Singh, "Personal Productivity and Locus of Control," *Sapience* (2017), accessed March 25, 2017, http://sapience.net/186-771-personal -productivity-locus-of-control.

3. Robert Parmer, "Locus of Control Is Alive and Well in the Workplace," *Thought Catalog* (February 20, 2015), accessed March 25, 2017, http:// thoughtcatalog.com/robert-parmer/2015/02/locus-of-control-is-alive-and -well-in-the-workplace.

4. Carol Sanford, "Feedback and Accountability on a Collision Course," *At Work: Stories of Tomorrow's Workplace* 5 (Sept/Oct 1996): 5, accessed March 29, 2017, www.CarolSanford.com.

5. Carol Sanford, *The Responsible Business: Reimagining Sustainability and Success* (San Francisco: Josey-Bass, 2011).

Chapter 4

1. Jeffrey Hollender, "Giving Up the CEO Seat," *Harvard Business Review*, March 2010 (Reprint R1003).

2. Jeffrey Hollender interviewed by Don Knauss, "Environmental Demand Drives Eco-friendly Products," PBS News Hour (August 15, 2008),

accessed April 28, 2017, http://www.pbs.org/newshour/bb/environment
-july-dec08-greengoods_08-15/.

Chapter 5

1. Ray Williams, "Why 'Constructive Feedback' Doesn't Improve Performance,"
   Psychology Today (November 26, 2011), accessed March 25, 2017, www
   .psychologytoday.com/blog/wired-success/201111/why-constructive
   -feedback-doesnt-improve-performance.
2. Grant Lichtman, "Is Dissonance an Enemy or Driver of Creative Problem
   Solving?" (October 6, 2016), accessed March 25, 2017, www.grantlichtman
   .com/is-dissonance-an-enemy-or-driver-of-creative-problem-solving.
3. Penny Tompkins and James Lawley, "Cognitive Dissonance and Creative
   Tension—The Same or Different?" *The Clean Collection* (October 3, 2009),
   accessed March 25, 2017, www.cleanlanguage.co.uk/articles/articles/262/1
   /Cognitive-Dissonance-and-Creative-Tension/Page1.html.
4. Matthew Panzarino, "Watch Steve Jobs Brainstorm with the NeXT Team
   in this Fascinating Video," TNW (The Next Web) (November 20, 2011),
   accessed March 25, 2017, https://thenextweb.com/shareables/2011/11/20
   /watch-steve-jobs-brainstorm-with-the-next-team-in-this-fascinating
   -video/#.tnw_74zytlsh. **Note:** Panzarino put "Brainstorm" in the title, but
   brainstorming is not what Jobs is doing here. He adds lots of structure,
   frameworks, and clean, externally facing questions, particularly when looking at differentiation.
5. Abby Bartholomew, "Behaviorism's Impact on Advertising: Then and Now,"
   Digital Commons, (University of Nebraska-Lincoln, 2013), accessed March
   25, 2017, http://digitalcommons.unl.edu/cgi/viewcontent.cgi?article=1042&
   context=journalismdiss.
6. Daniel Pink, *Drive: The Surprising Truth about What Motivates Us* (New
   York: Riverhead Books, 2009).
7. John Sullivan, "The Top 50 Problems with Performance Appraisals," TLNT
   Talent Management and HR (January 31, 2011), accessed March 25, 2017, www
   .eremedia.com/tlnt/the-top-50-problems-with-performance-appraisals.
8. Chris Joseph, "Problems with Performance Evaluations," *Chron* (The Houston
   Chronicle website, n.d.), accessed March 25, 2017, http://smallbusiness
   .chron.com/problems-performance-evaluations-1256.html.
9. Carol Sanford, *The Responsible Business: Reimagining Sustainability and
   Success* (San Francisco: Jossey-Bass, 2011).

10. Gregory Ciotti, "Why Steve Jobs Never Listened to His Customers," *HelpScout* (March 6, 2013), accessed March 25, 2017, www.helpscout.net /blog/why-steve-jobs-never-listened-to-his-customers.

11. Gerald Zaltman, *How Customers Think: Essential Insights into the Mind of the Market* (Boston: Harvard Business School Publishing, 2003).

Chapter 10

1. Carol Sanford's private notes from a closed meeting with Charles G. Krone in 1992.

2. Unless stated otherwise, all examples in this chapter are based on Carol Sanford's direct interaction or work experience with the company.

3. Brian Spiegel, "What Kind of Planes Does Southwest Airlines Fly?" *USA Today* (Travel Tips, n.d.), accessed March 27, 2017, http://traveltips.usatoday .com/kind-planes-southwest-airlines-fly-62394.html.

4. Gary Hamel and Bill Breen, *The Future of Management* (Boston: Harvard Business School Publishing, 2009).

Chapter 11

1. David Thau and Carol Sanford, "TRE—The Responsible Entrepreneur—David Thau," interview by Carol Sanford (April 27, 2015), accessed March 27, 2017, http://carolsanford.com/2015/04/tre-the-responsible-entrepreneur -david-thau.

Carol Sanford
Regenerative Business Offerings

CAROL SANFORD, Executive in Residence and Senior Fellow in Social Innovation at Babson College, is a keynote speaker and educator who inspires, challenges, and educates business leaders and businesspeople in all industries.

Regenerative Business Keynotes

Carol's keynotes are often called "original," "counterintuitive," and "game changing." She questions and challenges not only outdated ways of working but also those at the top of current best practices lists. Courageous Fortune 500 CEOs and leaders of recognized entrepreneurial businesses embrace her decades-long vetted methodology. Her own practice of forty years has provided her with extensively researched, powerful stories from diverse industries on four continents. Her contrarian approach challenges leaders to rethink everything they currently know about leadership, management, and work design, including best practices.

Carol has been described as a visionary whose shocking, profound, and easy-to-understand ideas can be put to use immediately. Her keynotes offer a pathway to extraordinary results.

To learn more about keynotes, visit www.CarolSanford.com.

Regenerative Business Educational Offerings

Carol Sanford is dedicated to growing the capacity of people and organizations to work in ways that align human development with business development. Disruptive, evolutionary growth makes a business resilient, agile, and innovative in a dynamic world, which is the purpose of a regenerative business.

To support these ends, Carol has created longstanding SEED communities and an in-house program through the Carol Sanford Institute that enable business leaders, businesspeople, and systems change agents to develop a sophisticated understanding of the regenerative business approach.

SEED Communities

Three SEED communities—for entrepreneurs (small businesses), impact investors (financial champions), and change agents (individuals with a professional practice)—initiate and lead revolutionary outcomes. Each works with Carol's innovation-sourced methodologies and developmental approach to doing business. Within the communities, powerful resourcing by peer groups enables members to develop their businesses, colleagues, and investments, which creates beneficial effects for all of the stakeholders in their work.

Visit www.SEED-communities.com.

The Carol Sanford Institute

The Carol Sanford Institute is a strategic innovation and alignment organization that offers a paradigm-shifting framework to leaders at Fortune 500 business units and entrepreneurially minded businesses to think innovatively and disruptively. This in-house program for executive education has been fully tested for decades with Carol's clients, and its track record is impeccable. The framework weaves together eighteen questions that must be asked in order for a business to become nondisplaceable in its market: six for revealing a compelling and unique strategic direction that cannot be replicated by others, six to develop leadership for change within the business and externally in the world, and six focused on the design of business structures, systems, and management processes. Collectively, all eighteen questions foster development of the acumen necessary to increase a current business's capacity and evolve it to become a regenerative business.

To learn more about the institute, visit www.CarolSanfordInstitute.com.

The Regenerative Business Summit and the Regenerative Business Prize

The Regenerative Business Summit is an annual event, focused on designing engagement among executives by utilizing seven *first principles* of regeneration. The summit includes no plenary speakers or panels. Instead, participants work together in small peer groups, using regenerative frameworks and processes to develop their professional capabilities and their business's regenerative capacity.

If you are an executive with fiduciary responsibility, please apply to Carol Sanford at www.The RegenerativeBusinessSummit.com for an invitation to attend the summit.

You may also wish to download information on the Regenerative Business Prize, including the Prize Report. The learning experiences of judges and contestants reveal a great deal about regenerative business practice and the development of regenerative capacity.

To learn more about the summit and prize, visit www.TheRegenerative BusinessSummit.com.

Index

Would you like your people to read this book?

If you would like to discuss how you could bring these ideas to your team, we would love to hear from you. Our titles are available at competitive discounts when purchased in bulk across both physical and digital formats. We can offer bespoke editions featuring corporate logos, customized covers, or letters from company directors in the front matter can also be created in line with your special requirements.

We work closely with leading experts and organizations to bring forward-thinking ideas to a global audience. Our books are designed to help you be more successful in work and life.

For further information, or to request a catalogue, please contact:
business@johnmurrays.co.uk
sales-US@nicholasbrealey.com (North America only)

Nicholas Brealey Publishing is an imprint of
John Murray Press.